Educational
Metamorphoses

Educational Metamorphoses

Philosophical Reflections on Identity and Culture

Jane Roland Martin

ROWMAN & LITTLEFIELD PUBLISHERS, INC.
Lanham • Boulder • New York • Toronto • Plymouth, UK

The acknowledgments section of this book constitutes an official extension of the copyright page.

ROWMAN & LITTLEFIELD PUBLISHERS, INC.

Published in the United States of America
by Rowman & Littlefield Publishers, Inc.
A wholly owned subsidiary of The Rowman & Littlefield Publishing Group, Inc.
4501 Forbes Boulevard, Suite 200, Lanham, Maryland 20706
www.rowmanlittlefield.com

Estover Road
Plymouth PL6 7PY
United Kingdom

Copyright © 2007 by Jane Roland Martin

British Library Cataloguing in Publication Information Available

Library of Congress Cataloging-in-Publication Data
Martin, Jane Roland, 1929–
  Educational metamorphoses : philosophical reflections on identity and culture / Jane Roland Martin.
    p. cm.
  Includes index.
  ISBN-13: 978-0-7425-4672-1 (cloth : alk. paper)
  ISBN-10: 0-7425-4672-1 (cloth : alk. paper)
  ISBN-13: 978-0-7425-4673-8 (pbk. : alk. paper)
  ISBN-10: 0-7425-4673-X (pbk. : alk. paper)
  1. Education—Social aspects. 2. Identity (Psychology)—Social aspects. I. Title.
  LC191.M267 2007
  306.43'2—dc22   2006020251

Printed in the United States of America

♾™ The paper used in this publication meets the minimum requirements of American National Standard for Information Sciences—Permanence of Paper for Printed Library Materials, ANSI/NISO Z39.48-1992.

To Mary Elizabeth Woods
(1930–2005)

Contents

List of Cases in Order of Appearance

Character	Source
Anthony Swofford	*Jarhead*, Anthony Swofford
Sandra Bartky	*Femininity and Domination*, Sandra Bartky
Alice Walker	*In Search of Our Mothers Gardens*, Alice Walker
Wilma Mankiller	*Mankiller*, Wilma Mankiller
Esmeralda Santiago	*Almost a Woman* and *The Turkish Lover*, Esmeralda Santiago
Heidi Bud	*Daughter of Danang*, PBS documentary
Donaldo Macedo	Interview

Introduction

One morning in the early 1970s a young Irish American from South Boston, the first in his family to attend college, knocked on the door of my office at the University of Massachusetts in Boston to say that he was leaving school. "I didn't want to go without telling you why. Last night when I was drinking beer with my buddies it came to me—it just came to me—that if I keep studying philosophy I won't be able to talk to them any more. We'll have nothing to say to each other. I like my friends and I like my family. I don't want to lose them."

The thought of that young man's deciding to forego a higher education in order to preserve his friendships and, ultimately, an entire way of life still haunts me. It is the reason I began collecting case studies of what I have come to call "educational metamorphoses." It is, indeed, the reason behind this book.

Throughout history and across cultures education, defined broadly, has changed the way we humans walk, talk, dress, behave, view the world, and live our lives. In other words, it has utterly transformed us. Nonetheless, current thinking often pictures it as nothing more than a producer of small, incremental changes in a person's knowledge or skill. Using cases drawn from fact and fiction, this book shows what a powerful maker and shaper of human lives education really is

On the day it dawned on me that George Bernard Shaw's play *Pygmalion* dramatizes my student's plight, I had in hand my first example of an educational metamorphosis. At the time I simply recognized that my student, like Shaw's Eliza Doolittle, was undergoing a radical change of identity: one due not to the wave of a wand or the administration of drugs, but to education. After seeing the film *Educating Rita* I added a second item to the collection of case studies that I still did not know I was amassing. And I happened on my third example when in 1982 I read Richard Rodriguez's memoir *Hunger of Memory*.

It was only when I was invited to teach a course in the undergraduate honors program at my university that it occurred to me that the interesting narratives I had been collecting during the twenty years since that encounter in my office were, in effect, instances of whole person transformations brought about by education. The heroes and heroines of these stories were a diverse lot: Eliza, Rita, and Richard Rodriguez for starters; but also Malcolm X; Ildefonso, a twenty-seven-year-old Mexican-American man without language; Victor, the Wild Boy of Aveyron; and I. B. Singer's Yentl. As the class progressed I realized that every single one of my cases was, like Shaw's play, a variation on the story about the sculptor Pygmalion and his statue Galatea that the Roman poet Ovid told in the book he called *Metamorphoses*.

Just as that course turned what until then had seemed to me to be a casual cluster of narratives into a coherent collection of cases, a book about the young boy whom Arctic explorer Robert Peary brought to New York City from the Polar North expanded my understanding of educational metamorphoses. Minik's case made me see that these phenomena have both an "inner" and an "outer" dimension. On the one hand they are personal transformations or identity changes; and on the other, they are culture crossings.

Some may be inclined to think that educational metamorphoses are rare events that only happen to extraordinary people living in exceptional circumstances. I tend to agree that if this were a static society and a stable time, far fewer educational metamorphoses would occur. In a world with closed borders, unwavering ethnic identities, fixed gender roles, frozen race and class relations, an unchanging technology, and a petrified economic system, people would have relatively little desire to change, nor would there be need to do so. But our world is in flux. The electronic revolution, the emergence of a global economy, the waves of immigration, the breakdown of class and gender barriers, and the myriad liberation movements: these and more have unmoored traditional social, economic, and cultural relations. In consequence, educational metamorphoses are now daily events.

Small wonder that over the years I have encountered educational metamorphoses everywhere. Small wonder that the sources of the cases in this book range from histories, memoirs, and autobiographical essays to dramas, novels, and television documentaries. Even so, if educational metamorphoses were unproblematic occurrences they would command little interest. But the case studies I have collected reveal that the great changes education brings about can be for the better or the worse. Malcolm X experienced a glorious whole person transformation that turned him from a Harlem pimp and drug dealer into a leader of his people, but he had earlier undergone a metamorphosis that had changed him from a model schoolboy into that selfsame pimp and drug dealer. Ildefonso started out as a despondent languageless man and became a confident speaker of American Sign Language, but other men his age have begun as relatively well-adjusted, peaceful citizens only to turn into disaffected participants in terrorist actions.

Can unwanted or undesirable educational transformations be avoided? Can policies and practices be devised to alleviate the alienation, fear, guilt, and shame that so often accompany even those metamorphoses that represent improvement? Not if the very existence of these radical changes of identity is barely acknowledged, and not if their dual character remains hidden from view. Developing an account of the often unruly metamorphoses that education brings about in individuals, this book seeks to expand understanding of education's role in human lives. Drawing attention to everyday phenomena that have all too often been ignored, it hopes to convince readers that education is one of the fundamental determinants of the human condition.

1

Rereading the
Pygmalion Myth

OVID'S "PYGMALION"

According to ancient myth, a sculptor named Pygmalion took a block of ivory and made of it such a beautiful figure of a woman that he fell in love with his own work of art.[1] So great was his passion that he draped his statue in the robes of a queen and showered it with kisses. Then, when the day of the Feast of Venus arrived, Pygmalion prayed fervently to the gods to give him a wife as lovely as his work of art. Hearing his plea and knowing what Pygmalion really wanted, the goddess Venus intervened. Lo and behold, when the sculptor returned home and once again caressed his ivory statue, she came to life.

Throughout the ages this story has been read as a myth of love, and so it is. But it is also a myth of creation. As the god Zeus created the woman Pandora, the man Pygmalion created a work of art in the form of a woman called Galatea. And it goes without saying that the tale contained in Book Ten of Ovid's *The Metamorphoses* is a myth of transformation. As Philomen and Baucis only had time to cry "Farewell, dear companion" before becoming an oak and a linden growing from a single trunk; as Daphne was turned into a laurel tree while fleeing Apollo's amorous advances; so Pygmalion, after praying to Venus, had merely to lie beside his statue and whisper endearments for it to become flesh and blood.

Love story, creation myth, transformation tale: Ovid's "Pygmalion" can be read in these three ways and one more. The philosopher George Santayana once wrote that the appeal of myths lies in their applicability to things known.[2] Part of the great appeal of Ovid's poem lies in the fact that it can also be understood as a myth about the power of education to form and transform human lives. This is the way George Bernard Shaw interpreted it when he wrote his play *Pygmalion*.[3]

Shaw is not given enough credit. Everyone knows that education can transform people. Yet how often is it portrayed as no more than a matter of small, incremental changes! Everyone knows that even the very best education can be an unruly affair and is almost always an unpredictable one. Yet how often have attempts been made to place its myriad aspects under tight control! Everyone knows that education elicits joy and heartbreak. Yet how often has it been seen as mundane and prosaic! To read Ovid's tale about Pygmalion as a story of education is to begin to set the record straight. Shaw knew—and *Pygmalion*, his play about the transformation of Cockney flower girl Eliza Doolittle into an English "lady" at the hands of linguist Henry Higgins demonstrates—that education is so powerful a force that it can transform not merely what an individual knows but who that person is.

Attempts to reduce education to its lowest common denominator are legion. One expert counts the number of years of schooling; another calculates how many grade levels have been completed; a third reckons up the hours devoted to homework or to the number of books read, math problems solved, spelling words memorized; and someone invariably wants to know how many correct answers were given on a test. True, when a person like Eliza undergoes a metamorphosis, he or she will very likely have accumulated a quantity of new knowledge and skill. Nonetheless, the radical transformations that come about through education are not necessarily the outcomes of schooling and cannot be equated with simple increases in learning. Although these great changes may not be quite so dramatic as Daphne's into a tree or as a caterpillar's into a butterfly, an individual who undergoes one becomes a new person. Eliza is not a better flower girl at the end of Shaw's play any more than Galatea is a bigger or better statue when Ovid's poem is done. They have both experienced a thoroughgoing change of being.

Shaw also knew that education is uncertain and often unpredictable. If a block of ivory can become Galatea, what might she in turn become? According to Ovid, Venus attended the wedding of Pygmalion and Galatea and blessed them both, and nine months later a girl was born to them— Paphos by name. But suppose Pygmalion bullies Galatea. Suppose she begins to resent the fact that a woman's work is never done. Suppose she has the opportunity to go to school. Almost anything might happen to Galatea after the birth of Paphos and, if truth be told, almost anything might also happen to Shaw's flower girl once she turns into a lady.

Shaw delighted in comparing the process of education to that of sculpture. To be sure, Henry Higgins tends to treat Eliza's education as a scientific experiment. Nevertheless, he continually envisions himself as a creative artist. "You have no idea how frightfully interesting it is to take a human being and change her into a quite different human being," he tells his mother (53). And to Eliza he says, "By George, Eliza, I said I'd make a woman of you; and I have" (88).

Educators are sometimes likened to gardeners. As the latter provide the conditions in which seeds turn into flowering plants, educators are said to arrange the environment so that the inherent capacities of their students can develop. According to this metaphor of growth, with proper attention the members of each new generation will turn into mature versions of their young selves in the manner of seeds, bulbs, and rosebuds. The imagery of Ovid's Pygmalion story attributes to education the very different, far larger task of shaping human lives.

It is tempting to say that being a lady is latent or inherent in Eliza from the start. How else could she become one? Aristotle believed that an acorn strives, as it were, to perfect itself as an oak, just as a rosebud tends or aims at the full realization of being a rose. Is not Eliza's metamorphosis best described as a striving to perfect the form appropriate to her?

It is legitimate to say that being an oak is latent or inhering in an acorn because acorns do not turn into maples or hemlocks, roses or tulips. Those that take root and grow, turn into oaks. In Aristotle's terminology, the shape of an oak is "the form" the species takes. There is, however, no "English lady form" for the human species; indeed, not even one for its female population. Of course Eliza the flower girl has the potentiality to become a lady, and not all things

do possess this. For instance, a zebra does not and, barring a gender change, neither does Henry Higgins. But she has lots of other
potentialities as well, among them being a scientist, a figure skater,
and a hardened criminal.

Why does Eliza not turn into one or more of these other beings?
Why only into a lady? Ladyhood is no more predetermined for
Eliza than it is foreordained that Pygmalion's block of ivory will
become a statue of a woman. No woman statue inheres in his block
of ivory in the way oakhood inheres in an acorn. Rather, the statue
eventually named Galatea is created by Pygmalion. Similarly, Eliza
becomes a lady not because ladyhood exists in her in latent form
and merely has to unfold. She reaches that end state by virtue of
the education she receives at Wimpole Street. This education does
not develop some *preexisting* lady capacity of hers. On the contrary,
it fosters *brand new* capacities in her—for example, the ability to
speak like a duchess—ones that in their turn make it possible for
her to become a lady.[4]

And Shaw knew what Ovid perhaps did not: that the great transformations education brings about in people have a cultural as well
as a personal or psychological dimension. Eliza does not simply become a different person. She becomes that cultural artifact known
as a late nineteenth—or perhaps early twentieth—century English
lady. Had she been born in Ovid's Rome she could have experienced a whole person transformation, but she could not possibly
have turned into the person she does. Moreover, Shaw puts culture-
crossing language into Eliza's mouth when he has her say to Higgins, "You told me, you know, that when a child is brought to a foreign country, it picks up the language in a few weeks, and forgets
its own. I am a child in your country. I have forgotten my own language and can speak nothing but yours" (80).

Following Shaw's lead, this book considers Ovid's tale a foun-
dational myth of education. But it goes much further than Shaw
went. By treating his play and the many other variations on the
Pygmalion theme in fact and fiction as case studies of educational
metamorphoses, this book reveals that education has transformed
almost every one of us from a creature of nature to a member of human culture. It discovers that a human life is a series of whole person or identity transformations brought about by education. And it
shows that because these great changes constitute crossings from

one culture or cultural group to another, they tend to be fraught with alienation, inner conflict, accusations of betrayal, and anxieties about going home again.

How often education is regarded as a tedious, humdrum affair: as inevitable perhaps as death and taxes, but of little intrinsic interest! Even if our lives were like those led by caterpillars and we underwent just one great metamorphosis in our lifetimes, this assessment would not be justified. But one of the many ways in which we differ from those marvelous creatures is that the driving force behind our metamorphoses is education. That is why we are subject not just to one but to any number of whole person changes. And it is also why we ought not to underestimate the power of education.

Casting education in a new light, this rereading of Ovid reveals it to be a major determinant of the human condition—as fundamental in its way as politics and economics are in theirs. For our Pygmalion tales demonstrate that it is not only fictional characters like Galatea and Eliza Doolittle who undergo radical whole person metamorphoses. They make it clear that every human being is repeatedly transformed.

SHAW'S VARIATION ON OVID'S THEME

In Ovid's rendition of the myth, after hearing Pygmalion say, "Give me a lady/Who is as lovely as my work of art,"[5] Venus grants his wish. Portraying Eliza Doolittle's transformation by linguist Henry Higgins from a "squashed cabbage leaf" (11) into a lady as a scientific experiment, Shaw represents her education as due to human labor rather than supernatural intervention. No god or goddess comes to Professor Higgins's rescue. Nor, for that matter, does he produce his changes by performing surgery on Eliza or administering drugs.

Shaw's play also shows an educational metamorphosis to be a gradual process, although not necessarily an easy or comfortable one. Once Venus intervenes, it takes but a moment for Galatea to come to life. As soon as the gods decide their time has arrived, Philomen and Baucis see each other putting forth leaves. "When Gregor Samsa awoke one morning from troubled dreams, he found himself transformed in his bed into a monstrous insect," wrote

Franz Kafka in *The Metamorphosis*.[6] These radical changes resemble the kind that evolutionary theorists call "saltational": rather than a new state of being emerging gradually, this type of change is a sudden, discontinuous production. In contrast, Eliza's transformation takes place over an extended period of time. According to Professor Higgins's friend Colonel Pickering, who is on the scene from start to finish, "Every week—every day almost—there is some new change. We keep records of every stage—dozens of gramaphone disks and photographs" (55).

The records they keep are of Eliza's linguistic progress. But although language learning is the lynchpin of her metamorphosis, were Shaw's flower girl merely to learn to speak a different form of English, she would not turn into another person. Someone who undergoes an educational metamorphosis resembles a scientist who has lived through a scientific revolution. He or she learns to see a new "gestalt"—a new world that looks quite different from the old one.[7] This is exactly what happens to Eliza. Where once she took a half-crown to be a small fortune and believed she would lose her "character" if she spoke to a gentleman, now she sees a way of life appropriately furnished with leather slippers and Stilton cheese.

Changes in a scientist's perceptions make the world look different, and so too for Eliza. Although her former world may look the same to everyone else, her new ways of thinking and acting and feeling make it an unknown territory for her. Echoes of Eliza's predicament can be heard in many of our Pygmalion tales, and Shaw's portrayal of her as a kind of immigrant caught between two cultures also finds confirmation in them. But this is to get ahead of ourselves.

For now, it suffices to say that Eliza's metamorphosis is both a transformation of her whole identity—the complete appearance and character change demanded by the dictionary definition of a metamorphosis—and a class crossing that amounts to a culture crossing. Shaw shows her to be the beneficiary not merely of Higgins's language instruction but also of an informal, mostly hidden curriculum in the manners and morals of the social class she will enter. Thus, in addition to learning to speak like a duchess, Eliza learns to think, feel, and act like a lady: not in the relatively limited sense of being able to play the role while remaining a flower girl, but in a more far-reaching one. Her walk, talk, and dress; her table manners and standards of cleanliness; her behavior toward old friends; her self-image, self-confidence, and self-respect: all these change.

It should be added that Eliza's metamorphosis comes about through a decidedly social process. Higgins does not single-handedly turn his cockney protégé into a lady. She is the product of Higgins's housekeeper's numerous kindnesses and her daily reminders to Eliza of what to do and say, the positive lessons that Colonel Pickering unwittingly teaches by his very presence, the negative ones that Eliza's father transmits during his visits to Wimpole Street, the lessons she learns on her forays into "high" society, and the ones she learns from her suitor, Freddy Eynsford-Hill.

Shaw's variation on Ovid's myth may be a work of fiction but as our other Pygmalion tales testify, it sheds dazzling light on the process and the problems of becoming educated. It also addresses questions about education that even philosophers of the subject have shunned. For Shaw knew—and here he went far beyond Ovid—that the moral and social questions to which education gives rise are as profound as can be. Does Henry Higgins have the right to change Eliza so radically? Who if anyone has the right to transform another? Is it ethical to try to change a person without that individual's consent? Do educational metamorphoses necessarily entail loss? Are such changes always improvements over what came before? Once transformed by education, can a person go home again?

WHAT KIND OF CHANGE IS AN EDUCATIONAL METAMORPHOSIS?

That education entails change of some sort would seem to be self-evident. If, as the great American philosopher William James maintained, "experience is moulding us every moment,"[8] think how much change education produces. Yet from the time of the early Greeks, philosophers have debated the nature of change and have asked if change is even possible. You believe that Eliza Doolittle changes? A descendant of the ancient philosopher Parmenides will tell you that although the flower girl *seems* to you to change, she does not really do so because her *underlying reality* remains the same. On the other hand, a descendant of his opponent, Heraclitus, will insist that nothing remains the same.

The most remarkable fact about the metaphysical disagreements regarding change that arose in ancient Greece is that they persist to this day. The impasse need not detain us, however. So long as people can agree that Eliza's walk, talk, and all the rest are transformed over time—and who upon reading Shaw's play or seeing *My Fair Lady*, the musical based on it, can doubt this—they must also agree that the kinds of changes that make a difference to the way people lead their lives do occur. The question for us, then, is not: Can change occur? It is: What kind of change is an educational metamorphosis?

Shaw portrays Eliza's transformation as a gradual affair. In contrast, psychologists have described a phenomenon they call *quantum change*. In quantum changes an individual also becomes a different person.[9] But whereas Eliza's transformation takes a relatively long time—six months, to be exact—quantum changes happen quickly, sometimes almost instantaneously.

In addition, quantum changes are marked by the occurrence of some momentous internal event. First-person reports of being taken by surprise, breaking down in tears, hearing voices, having "aha!" experiences, gaining control of one's life, and instantly recognizing the truth bear this out. For Eliza, on the other hand, there is no mystical experience or lightning bolt of insight. There is simply Higgins's regimen for her, Colonel Pickering's good manners toward her, the housekeeper's protection of her, Wimpole Street's class environment, Freddy Eynsford-Hill's doglike devotion, and Eliza's own dogged persistence. To be sure, "aha" experiences and sudden changes can be components of educational metamorphoses. But they do not amount to this kind of whole person transformation in and of themselves.

Note that to call Eliza's a "whole" person or "complete" identity change is not to suggest that every single characteristic of hers changes. She appears to have been an honest and outspoken young woman before she arrived on Higgins's doorstep and she remains one after her metamorphosis.[10] Rather, the terms *whole* and *complete* are meant to convey that her transformation is not purely intellectual or cognitive. Much as John Dewey, one of the educational greats, spoke of "the whole child" when insisting that education has to do not only with the mind, "whole" and "complete" signify that when an individual undergoes an educational metamorphosis, his or her thinking, behavior, feelings, emotions, attitudes, values, and ways of being in the world all undergo radical change.

It should be added that to say that educational metamorphoses are gradual affairs does not mean that they are dull pedestrian events. There is nothing banal or humdrum about Eliza's transformation. As Shaw demonstrated, her gradual metamorphosis from flower girl to lady is the stuff of drama. It does mean, however, that quantum change is one kind of metamorphosis and educational metamorphosis is another.

It should also be noted that the term *change* refers both to a process that takes place over time and to the result of that process. In every case of change the condition or state that something is in after it undergoes a change process differs from the condition or state it is in before the change process occurs. A metamorphosis is distinguished by the fact that its *end state* is radically different from its *initial state*. The end state is not necessarily unexpected or unpredictable: the metamorphosis of a caterpillar into a butterfly may once have been an unanticipated occurrence but it no longer is. To say that a radical transformation has occurred is simply to say that the end state is qualitatively different from the initial state.

In both quantum changes and educational metamorphoses the end state is so different from the initial state as to be discontinuous with it. Eliza does not end up a flower girl with educated speech. She becomes a totally different person, a member of another culture. So too, a person who undergoes a quantum change becomes a brand new individual, although not a culture crosser. But quantum changes occur, as it were, sans change process: in particular, without any intervening education. The radically different end state will presumably have a cause, but this will be at most a limiting instance of a change process. In contrast, in an educational metamorphosis the change process known as learning precedes the radically different end state. Thus, for example, Eliza learns how to say her "a's," then her "o's," then her "h's." She also learns new pitches and rhythms for her speech as well as new ways of sitting, standing, walking, and behaving. And eventually she is a lady.

From this account of Eliza's learning process it might seem as if her metamorphosis conforms to a model of education as a series of small, incremental changes. But although an incremental model may capture some parts or aspects of the educational process by which she is transformed into a lady, it does not capture the transformation as a whole. Indeed, what makes Eliza's educational metamorphosis so breathtaking is the great gap that exists between the discrete, easily identifiable behavioral changes that enter into the process of her transformation and the radical difference that constitutes an end state in which she does not merely act like a lady but has become one. How, one wonders, can a process such as the one Eliza undergoes yield an end product so utterly different from her earlier state of being?[11]

What the mathematical models used by biologists in the last century did for ecology—namely, bring rigor to the discipline by stripping away the complexity of real life—incremental models do for education. Representing learning as a matter of small, discrete changes that, loosely speaking, add up to a larger change, they portray education as a wholly predictable and thoroughly manageable phenomenon. As those mathematical models tended to be caricatures of biological reality,[12] incremental models turn the complicated, nonlinear, unruly process of education into a pale imitation of itself. In the real world, a teacher's walk, talk, dress, and demeanor are apt to send powerful hidden messages, the setting in which an educational episode occurs is apt to produce unintended consequences, and other educational agents—perhaps the learner's family, perhaps television—are apt to affect learning as well. For the sake of simplicity, incremental models treat both the outside influences on deliberate educational episodes and the unintended learnings that occur within such episodes as fluctuations from the norm that are best ignored.

Failing to take into account the complexity of even the simplest educational transactions, incremental models of learning do not accommodate educational metamorphoses. To be sure, whole person transformations may include discrete, intended changes. But a new identity emerges in the course of an educational metamorphosis, something that is not simply the sum of the small discrete changes. To use an overworked metaphor, the resultant whole that represents the end state of an educational metamorphosis is more than the sum of its parts.

Yet are educational metamorphoses really more than the sum of their parts or do they merely appear to be more because too few of their parts are taken into account? Of course Eliza's becoming a lady is more than the sum of her learning to pronounce her vowels and her h's as a lady does. But is it more than the sum of her learning to walk, talk, dress, think, and behave like a lady? If it is not, then her transformation into a lady would seem to be an incremental process after all.

Is the only reason why educational metamorphoses do not conform to an incremental model that we lack the relevant knowledge? Were it possible to escape our finite human perspective and look at Eliza's transformation from an all-seeing standpoint, might we be able to specify enough steps in her learning process to make her having become a lady look like a continuous process of change from beginning to end? Or for that matter, were the human sciences more advanced than they now are, might they tell us all we need to know to reduce her metamorphosis to a series of small increments?

Shaw makes it clear that much of the behavior Eliza learns at Wimpole Street and its environs is not due to Higgins's efforts. But imagine now that Higgins is in fact the one who teaches Eliza the manners of a lady. Even if her learning is reducible to a series of discrete steps or events that he has designed, their sum total is still not the new person that Eliza becomes. At best, they add up to Eliza's knowing how to *act like* or *pass as* a new person. But although Eliza may have been at this state at one point in the transformational process, by the end of it she has gone far beyond "passing" as a lady to *being* one.

Given the present limitations on human knowledge, there is a great gap between what Eliza does or undergoes and what she becomes. Yet even if future research can fill in part of the gap, an analysis that reduces educational metamorphoses to a series of incremental changes will not suffice. For the ways of walking, talking, dressing, thinking, and the like that Eliza acquires in the course of her transformation—and also the traits and dispositions she sheds—are items of culture. To be sure, those portions of what may be called "cultural stock" are not included in the concept of "high" culture. But "high" culture is only one small part of the stock of human cultures.[13] In the broad sense of the term—the sense employed by anthropologists and sociologists—culture encompasses the institutions and practices, rites and rituals, beliefs and skills, attitudes and values, worldviews and localized modes of thinking and acting of *all* members of society over the *whole* range of contexts. This means that in addition to being more than the sum of its parts, Eliza's educational metamorphosis, like all educational metamorphoses, has an irreducible cultural component.

For several reasons, those who see children as raw material and educators as workers whose job it is to turn their charges into acceptable end products may find the idea of educational metamorphoses unsettling. To admit the existence of these phenomena is to acknowledge that things can happen to an individual in the course of becoming educated that could not have been predicted and that lie outside the educator's control. Could anyone have foreseen that Freddy would fall madly in love with Eliza or that she would triumph at the ball? Is Henry Higgins really able to control the actions of Colonel Pickering, let alone of Alfred P. Doolittle? Furthermore, the things that can happen to an individual in the course of becoming educated extend beyond the acquisition of new knowledge and skills to the formation of brand new cultural identities. And finally, the very existence of these phenomena will give pause too to those who think of education as a "Do X and you will get result Y" type of human engineering. For it signifies that even if you get Y when you do X, no one may know what will happen next. It reminds one that the dream of taming education and curbing its unruliness by bringing it under tight control is just that—a dream.

IS THE PYGMALION MYTH AN EDUCATION STORY?

In sum, an educational metamorphosis is a large-scale change—a whole person or complete identity change—that humans undergo, one that is aptly characterized as being greater than the sum of its parts. But although in this latter respect educational metamorphosis resembles quantum change, it differs from that form of personal transformation in important ways.

How many of us have undergone an educational metamorphosis, under what circumstances, and how often? The cases of Victor, the Wild Boy of Aveyron, and Genie, a young Los Angeles girl, both of which are discussed in chapter 2, leave little doubt that under normal circumstances we all undergo a whole person transformation at an early age—one we quickly forget. The life story of

Malcolm X to be considered in chapter 3 teaches, in its turn, that the metamorphosis each one of us experiences as a very young child is but the first of many transformations that an individual undergoes in a lifetime. The case presented in chapter 4 of Minik, a young Inuit boy, is one of many that supports Shaw's insight that a whole person transformation represents a journey into a different culture. And the varieties of educational metamorphoses recounted in chapter 5 suggest the wide range of conditions that can give rise to these great changes. But before specifically addressing questions about the scope and nature of educational metamorphoses, it behooves us to consider the insults, threats, unreasonable commands, bullying, browbeating, and mindless repetition to which Professor Higgins subjects Eliza Doolittle.

"Somebody is going to touch you, with a broom-stick, if you don't stop sniveling," he says to her the day she arrives at his residence on Wimpole Street (20). Mispronounce tea again and "you shall be dragged around the room three times by the hair of your head," he tells "this draggletailed guttersnipe" (20), "this unfortunate animal" (40) at her first lesson. It is generally assumed that education is a moral enterprise. In light of Higgins's scandalous behavior must we conclude that this most famous variation on Ovid's myth is not about education after all?

For the record, let it be known that although Professor Higgins does not pay Eliza compliments as Pygmalion does Galatea, he never lays a hand on her. In addition, although some might object to his way of talking to Eliza, on close inspection his behavior compares favorably to that of many teachers in fact and fiction.

The day Amy March, one of Louisa May Alcott's "little women," brought pickled limes to school to share with her friends her teacher struck her several times on the hand. He then further humiliated her by making her stand on a platform facing her classmates.[14]

Charles Dickens's David Copperfield tells us that his teacher, Mr. Creakle, is "an incapable brute." "Here I sit at the desk again," he says, "humbly watching his eye, as he rules a ciphering book for another victim whose hands have just been flattened by that identical ruler, and who is trying to wipe the sting out with a pocket-handkerchief."[15]

One may not approve Henry Higgins's treatment of Eliza; indeed, one might not wish to engage him to teach oneself or one's children. Nevertheless, Higgins's methods fall well within the boundaries of that thing Western culture calls education.[16] One has only to read George Orwell's memoir *Such, Such Were the Joys . . .* , or Marie Arana's *American Chica* to know that the portraits drawn by Alcott and Dickens are not figments of overwrought imaginations. Granted, works of art are not exact replicas of real life phenomena. The fact is, however, that fictional accounts converge with established educational practice.

Orwell, author of *Animal Farm* and *1984*, reported that the headmaster of his British boarding school would say, "Come along you useless little slacker. Come into the study. And then whack, whack, whack, whack, and back one would come, red-wealed and smarting . . . to settle down to work again."[17]

Peruvian-American writer Marie Arana described what happened to her brother when he got into a fight on his first day of primary school in Peru. "I'll show *you* what happens to troublemakers. Everyone take note! *Fijense* what happens to this uppity boy!" said George's teacher. She then "trotted George—still dangling from her hand—over to the closet, opened the door, and thrust him in. She turned the lock with a click, and whirled around."[18]

But to pursue the question at hand, let us suppose that Higgins's teaching methods are deemed morally objectionable. This does not negate the claim that Shaw's play is an education story. Yes, education is a moral enterprise. However, this is not to say that an educator by definition acts morally or that an educated person is necessarily a moral person. All it means is that education is one of those human practices to which moral judgments apply.[19]

The tendency to think of anything that goes under the title "education" as intrinsically praiseworthy is understandable. There is something comforting about the thought that education is by definition morally good and that whatever harm is done in its name is not really education but is socialization or indoctrination or conditioning or mere training. Yet to call whatever goes by the label "education" moral *by definition* is to deny the facts: it is to insist in the face of all the evidence that the physical and psychological abuse of children and the grossly unfair treatment some receive never occur in educational contexts. Or else it is to turn morality upside down by affirming that such patently unethical behavior conforms to the dictates of morality.

It is also comforting to think that education and moral improvement go hand in hand. Yet despite the fact that many of the finest educational thinkers the West has known have stressed the ideas of growth and development and the fact that these notions tend to imply improvement, this is not so.

Plato, one of the greatest philosophers of education in the Western tradition, agreed with Parmenides that to all intents and purposes, change is illusory. But other "greats" have placed growth and development at the very center of their educational theories. Saying, "Plants are shaped by cultivation, and men by education," Jean-Jacques Rousseau did just this.[20] John Dewey, in turn, defined education as "a continuous process of growth" and growth as "a continuous leading into the future."[21] And Alfred North Whitehead, who along with Rousseau and Dewey has been called one of the three great modern philosophers of education,[22] incorporated an evolutionary perspective into his overall thought and in his work on education spoke repeatedly of development.

The dictionary defines *develop* as "to bring to a more advanced or effective state." As it happens, although Higgins and Pickering think that the new condition Eliza's education has produced is an improvement over the old, she herself has doubts: "Oh! if I could only go back to my flower basket! I should be independent of both of you and father and all the world! Why did you take my independence from me? Why did I give it up? I'm a slave now, for all my fine clothes" (85). Her father questions the value of her new self too: "Undeserving poverty is my line. Taking one station in society with another, it's—it's—well, it's the only one that has any ginger to it, to my taste" (36).

There is no need to settle here the dispute about Eliza's fate. The relevant point is that neither education in general nor educational metamorphoses in particular always represents movement toward a more advanced state. In the case of metamorphoses, naturalist Maria Merian recognized this in the early eighteenth century, and two hundred years later it was acknowledged again by Kafka. Merian wrote, "It has happened to me more than once that the most beautiful caterpillars have transformed themselves into very ugly butterflies, and that there have emerged very beautiful ones from the ugliest caterpillars."[23] These discoveries greatly surprised her because the prevailing view of development was Aristotelian. Each individual member of a species was thought to strive to embody as perfectly as possible the form that species takes; thus, it was believed that a colt will develop into the best horse it can and an acorn into the most perfect oak tree.

Lest it be objected that even an ugly butterfly is in a more advanced state than the most beautiful caterpillar, there is Kafka's Gregor Samsa to be reckoned with. Who but another large insect would want to claim that Samsa, the hard-working bureaucrat, is in a less advanced state than Samsa the cockroach! And if it now be objected that Kafka did quite literally mean to say that Samsa the bureaucrat is less advanced than his successor, there is the case of Malcolm X, who in his teens was transformed from a model schoolboy to a Harlem hustler and pimp.

Let there be no mistake. The idea of change encompasses the development of criminals as well as heroes, totalitarian regimes as well as democracies, and cancer as well as good health. Similarly, the idea of education applies to new states of being whether good or bad, beneficial or detrimental. Insofar as the idea of growth shares connotations of advance or betterment with development, it is also misleading. Dewey considered growth a continuous leading into the future. Does Eliza's transformation into a lady lead into the future or cut it off? Shaw's play does not answer this question, nor should it. As our tales of Pygmalion repeatedly demonstrate, one mark of an educational metamorphosis is that it leaves us ignorant of what will happen next. When Merian conducted her investigations of insects, the dominant view of development was that the future should be deducible from the past.[24] Education's lack of predictability has a double aspect: the transformations themselves cannot be predicted in advance, and once they are achieved the future still cannot be foretold.

EDUCATION AS A SHAPER OF HUMAN LIVES

Just as the term *education* sometimes has moral overtones and sometimes not, it sometimes refers to a voluntary, deliberate activity whose aim is the acquisition of knowledge and understanding, and sometimes not. Definitions abound that turn education into a purely rational process: one whose participants always know what they are doing, do whatever they do voluntarily, and invariably act with conscious intent; and whose aims are strictly intellectual.[25] But these narrow formulas do not do justice to the broad scope of our subject. Our case studies substantiate that although some of the education a person receives over the course of a lifetime is a conscious, deliberate undertaking, some of it happens accidentally and occurs unbeknown to the educator or the learner.

So far as educational metamorphoses are concerned, although some of their components may fit these requirements, the whole person transformations that constitute them do not. Does Eliza know what she is doing when she asks Professor Higgins to teach her to speak like a lady? It is indisputable that she voluntarily puts herself in Higgins's charge. She does so because she believes—correctly, as it happens—that he can teach her to speak like a lady. But before the experiment begins Eliza has no idea of the work it will entail, no idea of the bruises her ego will suffer, no idea what the outcome will really be, no idea that once she arrives at her destination she will be an entirely different person and that there will be no turning back.

Is the end state of Eliza's educational metamorphosis merely a change in her knowledge and understanding? The new person she becomes as a result of the education she receives at Wimpole Street is not simply an intellect. She is a thinking, acting, feeling being. Treating flesh and blood people as if they were nothing but minds, definitions that reduce education to mental or cognitive attainments, dismiss our bodies from the scene. They also cast out our feelings and emotions, for these definitions tacitly assume that the human mind is the locus of rational processes only, and that feelings and emotions are fundamentally irrational.[26]

Once again, the tendency to reduce education to a voluntary, intentional, self-aware, and rational endeavor whose sole task is to give people knowledge and develop mental capacities is comprehensible. As incremental models dissipate concerns that education is an unruly, unpredictable phenomenon by giving the illusion of control, so do narrow intellectualistic definitions. With all parties to educational transactions knowing what they are doing and wanting to do what they are doing, it makes sense to believe that we can know what will happen next. With education's task restricted to the development of mind, there would seem to be no reason to fear that notoriously unruly aspects of the human condition, such as feelings, emotions, attitudes, and behavior, might get out of hand. Nonetheless, such definitions play fast and loose with the facts.

So much for the likes and dislikes, attitudes and values that are unconsciously picked up during formal spelling and geography lessons—what Dewey termed "collateral learning."[27] So much for the hidden curriculum of schooling in obedience and conformity documented by radical school reformers of the last century. So much for all those who use the term *education* to include child rearing as well as schooling, and to embrace informal and unintended learning and teaching.[28] And so much for the metamorphoses whose whole person transformations give shape to the lives we live.

Like incremental models of education, narrow definitions of the educational process and a belief that the objects of educational concern are minds divorced from bodies and devoid of feelings and emotions represent habits of thought that are not easily abandoned. But a rereading of the Pygmalion myth as an education story renders them obsolete.

We human beings are not blocks of ivory or finely sculpted statues. Yet when Ovid's tale is read together with Shaw's and the many other variations on the Pygmalion theme, it sheds wondrous light on the human condition. Bringing into focus education's power to shape and transform our lives, it serves as a reminder that every single one of us undergoes whole person or identity transformations that are also culture crossings, that these are not necessarily the products of schooling, that some of them are educative and others are miseducative, and that even the educative ones can be full of pain as well as joy.

In view of the centrality of educational metamorphoses to the human condition, it is rather a puzzlement that their existence is so often overlooked. The fact is, however, that even those philosophers, psychologists, and educators who have talked about the transformation of human individuals have not carried the idea through to its logical conclusion. In the midtwentieth century two social scientists published a book entitled *Pygmalion in the Classroom,* and it might be thought that this volume had thoroughly explored our subject.[29] But despite the title, Ovid's hero made only one entrance into the scene and that was on the very last page of the book; there was no recognizable Galatea in the volume, not even in the chapter that bore her name; and metamorphoses were not discussed. In the chapters of the present volume there are recognizable Pygmalions and Galateas galore, albeit in many different shapes, sizes, genders, classes, ethnicities, and colors. There are also whole person or identity transformations to spare, for each one of our variations on the Pygmalion theme represents a case study of an educational metamorphosis.

Lest there be any doubt, to underscore the prevalence and the power of educational metamorphoses does not entail the rejection of incremental models and narrow definitions of education. These latter have always been and will likely remain applicable to limited forms of education. To admit the centrality of educational metamorphoses may, however, require a shift of some magnitude—one might even venture to say a "transformation"—in many people's thinking. For our case studies leave little doubt that every last one of us is a different person from the newborn we once were. Indeed, they indicate that we have all experienced a series of educational metamorphoses between then and now.

We tend to think of the genes within us and the political and economic processes outside of us as the great forces affecting our lives. But genes are not destiny. They do not turn Eliza into a lady. Nor did they turn Victor into a French child; Malcolm Little into a school mascot, let alone into a Harlem hustler and then a leader of his people; Minik, the child from the Polar North, into an all-American boy; the young African-American girl born in rural Georgia named Alice Walker into a civil rights activist, let alone a world-renowned writer; or the young San Francisco housewife and mother named Wilma Mankiller into a chief of the Cherokee people. And although politics and economics surely entered into the whole person transformations of these individuals, those large-scale processes did not in and of themselves determine the precise form their metamorphoses took.

Education when defined broadly and seen as the shaper of whole persons and not just minds is the great force that accomplished this. Indeed, our cases reveal that educational metamorphoses function in human lives much as world historic events do in human history. As discoveries, inventions, wars, revolutions, and social movements give history its structure, the personal transformations or metamorphoses that each one of us experiences give form and shape to our lives.

NOTES

1. Ovid, *The Metamorphoses* (New York: Mentor Book, 1960), Book Ten.

2. George Santayana, *The Life of Reason* (New York: Charles Scribner's, 1953), 202.

3. George Bernard Shaw, *Pygmalion* (New York: New American Library, 1975). Page references appear in parentheses in the text.

4. "When the idea that development is due to some indwelling end which tends to control the series of changes passed through is abandoned, potentialities must be thought of in terms of consequences of interactions with other things." John Dewey, "The Influence of Darwinism on Philosophy," in *The Moral Writings of John Dewey*, ed. James Gouinlock (New York: Hafner Press, 1976), 40.

5. Ovid, *The Metamorphoses*, 282.

6. Franz Kafka, "The Metamorphosis," in *The Metamorphosis and Other Stories* (New York: Penguin Books, 1992), 64.

7. Cf. Thomas S. Kuhn, *The Structure of Scientific Revolutions* (Chicago: University of Chicago Press, 2nd ed., 1970), 112.

8. William James, *The Principles of Psychology*, vol. 1 (New York: Dover Publications, 1950), 234.

9. William R. Miller and Janet C'de Baca, *Quantum Change* (New York: Guilford Press, 2001).

10. Thus, the idea of an educational metamorphosis does not contradict hypotheses that attribute to infants an inborn temperament of character that endures for life. See, e.g., Jerome Kagan and Nancy Snidman, *The Long Shadow of Temperament* (Cambridge, MA: Harvard University Press, 2004).

11. For an interesting account of "learning as a whole" as opposed to "learning by steps," see Ikuta Kumiko, "What Are the Implications of the Teaching and Learning Method of Traditional Japanese Artistic Performances," *Bildung und Erziehung*, vol. 53, no. 5 (December 2000), 429–39.

12. For a fuller discussion of such models see James Gleick, *Chaos* (New York: Penguin Books, 1987), 60.

13. For an extended discussion of the concept of cultural stock see Jane Roland Martin, *Cultural Miseducation* (New York: Teachers College Press, 2002).

14. Louisa May Alcott, *Little Women* (Boston: Little, Brown, 1936), chap. 7.

15. Charles Dickens, *David Copperfield* (New York: Walter J. Black, n.d.), 119.

16. For other novels that portray teaching in this same light see, e.g., Charlotte Bronte, *Jane Eyre* (New York: Signet Books, 1997); Richard Llewellyn, *How Green Was My Valley* (New York: Simon and Schuster, 1997).

17. George Orwell, "Such, Such Were the Joys . . ." *The Orwell Reader* (New York: Harcourt Brace, 1984), 427.

18. Marie Arana, *American Chica* (New York: Dial Press, 2001), 211–12. Cf. Mark Mathabane, *Kaffir Boy* (New York: Simon and Schuster, 1986).

19. See John I. Goodlad, Corinne Mantle-Bromley, and Stephen John Goodlad, *Education for Everyone* (San Francisco: Jossey-Bass, 2004), for a similar point.

20. Jean-Jacques Rousseau, *Emile* (New York: Basic Books, 1979), 38. For a critique of Rousseau's natural growth metaphor, see Jane Roland Martin, *Reclaiming a Conversation* (New Haven, CT: Yale University Press, 1985), chap. 3.

21. John Dewey, *Democracy and Education* (New York: Macmillan, 1961), 54, 56.

22. Robert S. Brumbaugh and Nathaniel M. Lawrence, *Philosophers on Education: Six Essays on the Foundations of Western Thought* (Boston: Houghton Mifflin, 1963).

23. Quoted in Marina Warner, *Fantastic Metamorphoses, Other Worlds* (Oxford: Oxford University Press, 2002), 79.

24. Warner, *Metamorphoses*, 79.

25. See, e.g., R. S. Peters, "What Is an Educational Process?" in *The Concept of Education*, ed. R. S. Peters (New York: Humanities Press, 1967), 3ff.

26. For an extended discussion of this point, see Jane Roland Martin, *Changing the Educational Landscape* (New York: Routledge, 1994), chap. 9.

27. John Dewey, *Experience and Education* (New York: Macmillan, 1963), 48.

28. After distinguishing a broad and a narrow sense of the term *education* and aligning the narrow sense with intentionality and the development of knowledge and understanding, the influential twentieth-century philosopher of education R. S. Peters deemed the broad sense philosophically uninteresting. R. S. Peters, "Education and the Educated Man," in *A Critique of Current Educational Aims*, ed. R. F. Dearden and R. S. Peters (London: Routledge and Kegan Paul, 1972).

29. Robert Rosenthal and Lenore Jacobson, *Pygmalion in the Classroom* (New York: Holt, Rinehart and Winston, 1968).

2

The Journey from
Nature to Human Culture

VICTOR'S CASE

Although it was Shaw's genius to read the Pygmalion myth as an education story, his variation on Ovid's theme does not do the original myth full justice. In Ovid's tale there are two metamorphoses: first a block of ivory turns into a statue and then that statue becomes a flesh and blood woman. In Shaw's *Pygmalion* there is just one. Shaw gives a compelling portrait of Eliza's transformation from flower girl to lady, but he lets Eliza's first great metamorphosis from newborn to young girl drop out of the picture.

"From the moment [man] is thrown into this world he is responsible for everything he does," wrote Existentialist philosopher Jean Paul Sartre.[1] One has only to look at a human newborn to know that this is not true. As contemporary anthropology reminds us, at birth we human beings are "barely human and utterly unsocialized"[2]; indeed, we are "incomplete or unfinished animals who complete or finish ourselves through culture."[3] In particular, an infant cannot speak, walk upright, or control its excretions, and it certainly has no understanding of social duties, responsibilities, or morals.

The flower girl Professor Higgins meets in Covent Garden may lack the accomplishments and polish of a lady but she is not like

the statue imagined by Rousseau. "Let us suppose," wrote Rousseau in Book I of *Emile,*

> that a child had at his birth the stature and the strength of a grown
> man, that he emerged, so to speak, fully armed from his mother's
> womb as did Pallas from the brain of Jupiter. This man-child would
> be a perfect imbecile, an automaton, an immobile and almost insen-
> sible statue. He would see nothing, hear nothing, know no one,
> would not be able to turn his eyes toward what he needed to see. Not
> only would he perceive no object outside of himself, he would not
> even relate any object to the sense organ which made him perceive
> it: the colors would not be in his eyes; the sounds would not be in his
> ears; the bodies he touched would not be on his body; he would not
> even know that he had one.[4]

Long before the action of Shaw's *Pygmalion* begins, Eliza learned
to hear sounds, recognize colors, walk, talk, dress herself, and so
on. In other words, offstage she underwent the metamorphosis we
all undergo as we are transformed from creatures of nature to
members of human culture.

What better way to grasp the import of the event represented in
Ovid's tale by the sculpting of a statue out of a block of ivory than
to examine the case of Victor, the Wild Boy of Aveyron.[5] Emile was
published in 1762. Thirty-five years later, Victor came out of the
woods near Aveyron, France. One year after that he was caught
and taken to a nearby village where he was put on display in the
public square. From there he managed to escape, only to be cap-
tured and placed in the keep of an old widow. Again he ran away
and then, on January 8, 1800, he walked of his own accord into the
workshop of a dyer named Vidal. On Day 2 of Victor's life in human society a government official took him in charge and on Day
3 the boy was shipped off to an orphanage.

In a letter written two weeks after Victor's arrival, an orphanage
administrator wrote:

> The child appears to be twelve years of age at most. He is nice look-
> ing. His eyes are dark and full of life. He searches incessantly for a
> means of escape. We let him out this morning in a field next to the
> orphanage. He took to running on all fours. If we had not followed
> him closely and overtaken him, he would soon have reached the
> mountain and disappeared. He trots when walking. We made him a
> gown of gray linen. He does not know how to get it off, but this gar-

ment annoys him greatly. We have just let him free in the garden. Wanting to escape, he tried to break one of the strips of wood in the gate. He never speaks. When he is given potatoes, he takes as many as his pretty little hands can hold. If the potatoes are cooked (he prefers them thus), he peels them and eats them like a monkey. He has a pleasing laugh. If you take his potatoes away from him, he lets out sharp cries. Constans believes that he is deaf. We have just convinced ourselves to the contrary; at most he is hard of hearing. (10)

Six months later the Wild Boy, as Victor was then called, was sent to Paris where he was greeted with fanfare. In that capital of culture he was observed by scientists and philosophers who anticipated that with his help they would answer the central question of the Enlightenment—*What is the Nature of Man?* But by the end of the year, all but one or two of these men had concluded that the Wild Boy had nothing to teach them about man's nature or even about the relative importance of nature and nurture in man's development. The child was an idiot and therefore uneducable.

The main dissenter from this dismal assessment was Jean-Marc-Gaspard Itard, who on the last day of 1800 was appointed resident physician at the Institute for Deaf-Mutes. There he undertook a scientific experiment designed to prove that the child he named Victor could after all acquire human language. Like Professor Higgins, Doctor Itard designed a formal training program whose raison d'être was language mastery. Eliza, however, had merely to master what amounted to a second language whereas in Victor's case first language learning was at stake.

As was true for Eliza, Victor's education encompassed much more than language acquisition. When the boy emerged from the woods, his walk was a trot and he ran on all fours. He ate only potatoes, raw chestnuts, and acorns. He defecated wherever he happened to be. He tore off his clothes and slept on the floor. He did not seem to hear people speak to him or cry out or play music although he could hear a walnut broken behind him, a dog barking, and a door opening. One year later Victor was still spending his time squatting in a corner of the garden or hiding in an attic. Thus, Itard reported:

When observed inside his own room he was seen swaying with tiring monotony, turning his eyes constantly toward the window, gazing sadly into space. If a stormy wind then chanced to blow, if the sun suddenly came from behind the clouds brilliantly illuminating the skies, he expressed an almost convulsive joy with clamorous peals of laughter, during which all his movements backward and forward very much resembled a kind of leap he would like to take, in order to break through the window and dash into the garden. Sometimes instead of these joyful emotions, he exhibited a kind of frantic rage, wrung his hands, pressed his closed fists to his eyes, gnashed his teeth audibly, and became dangerous to those who were near him. (100)

It is frequently said that we humans do not remember how we acquired language.[6] Nor do we remember learning to distinguish hot and cold, to recognize colors, to walk, or to use a spoon and fork. Indeed, once children are grown, it is hard to believe that they ever lacked these abilities. That is why Victor's case is so instructive. Forcing us to acknowledge what we ourselves would be like if we had never made the journey from nature to culture, it allows us to see that the metamorphosis Victor was denied when he was very young is one of the most significant events—perhaps *the* most significant—in *any* human life.

LANGUAGE AS THE MEASURE OF MAN

Victor's variation on the Pygmalion theme reveals the limits of incremental models of education. Itard's experiment lasted some five years. During that time the boy who everyone believed incapable of paying attention learned to be attentive, to reflect, and to rely on his memory. He also learned to compare, discern, judge, and communicate his wants in writing. In addition he learned to dress himself, ride in a carriage, eat a variety of foods with utensils, set the table, copy words in writing, and help Mme. Guérin, Itard's housekeeper, dress herself. Perhaps most important, Victor acquired a number of the feelings and sentiments associated with morality: in particular, gratitude, affection, remorse, and a sense of justice. And he learned to take pleasure in helping the people he was fond of, even going so far as to anticipate their needs.

Viewed singly, these accomplishments can be seen as a set or series of incremental learnings. Taken together they represent a whole person metamorphosis. An evaluator commissioned by the French government suggested that Victor be compared not with external standards but only with himself: "We should remember what he was when placed in the hands of this physician, see what he is now, *and consider the distance separating his starting point from the one he has reached*" (166, emphasis added). Do this, and rather than a collection of small changes we have a whole person transformation. Chronologically speaking, Victor was no infant when he walked out of the woods. Culturally speaking, he might well be considered one. When Itard took charge of him, the boy had yet to make the journey from nature to culture that all of us have done and that none of us can recall. By 1806 he was not a Wild Child but another person altogether.

If this be so, why was Itard's experiment considered a failure? Henry Higgins's fictional experiment lasted six months and has generally been regarded as a great success. Not so Itard's historical experiment.

The main question that commentators on Victor's case have asked over the years is, Why didn't he progress further intellectually and, above all, why didn't he acquire spoken language? At the time and over the centuries, people have also wondered: Did the problem lie in Itard's methods? Was Victor so old that his asocial habits were irreversible? Could he have been autistic?

Compare Victor with the flower girl, Eliza. Then the question of why he took so long to acquire language is apt: five years pass and his grasp of the French language remains slight. Recognize that when Itard took charge of Victor the boy had not yet undergone the metamorphosis from creature of nature to member of culture that Eliza experienced offstage as a young child. Then the issue of language acquisition no longer looms so large. Just as Ovid's sculptor created a statue out of the material at hand, Itard—with the assistance of Mme. Guérin—produced a child who, despite his limited linguistic skills, was recognizably French.

Compare Victor with himself and one can but marvel at the great change in him between 1801 and 1806. Granted, when sophisticated French society opened its doors to Victor his behavior left something to be desired. When he dined at a fashionable salon, the boy ate greedily, filled his pockets with goodies, and vanished. The next thing anyone knew he was

running across the lawn with the speed of a rabbit. To give himself more freedom of movement, he had stripped to his undershirt.

Reaching the main avenue of the part, which was bordered by huge
chestnut trees, he tore his last garment in two, as if it were simply
made of gauze; then, climbing the nearest tree with the ease of a
squirrel, he perched in the middle of the branches. (109)

Lest we forget, before Henry Higgins and company remade Eliza,
her behavior in high society also lacked polish. If at that point Professor Higgins had washed his hands of the affair, would she have
passed as a lady at an embassy ball? Surely not.

Whether Victor's transformation to a young man able to navigate high French society could have been achieved had the
government—or for that matter, private individuals—seen fit to
continue his education we will never know. For despite a recom-
mendation by the outside examiner that Victor's education be
continued, it was abandoned. A five-year initiation into human
culture is not so long when one thinks of the time it takes to in-
duct chronological infants and the fact that Victor was a very late
bloomer. Nevertheless, in 1806 the French government decided to
give Madame Guérin an allowance of 150 francs a year for his
care. And so Victor left Itard's charge and moved into her home
where he stayed until his death in 1828.

For all Henry Higgins's bullying and petulance, Eliza's story has
a triumphal ring. Despite Itard's many kindnesses, Victor's does
not. A boy comes out of the forest where he presumably was abandoned as a very young child. No one knows exactly why or when
this happened, but the upshot is that he possesses no social graces
or skills whatsoever. The boy is taken in charge and made the subject of a scientific experiment. Five years pass and the boy is a new
person. Nevertheless, he is once again abandoned. This time we
know why: his intellectual development has not progressed as the
experts believe it should have and, most damaging, he has not acquired spoken language.

Two hundred years later we need to ask why success in language
learning loomed so large in the minds of those who took an interest in Victor and why Victor's moral and emotional and physical
development mattered so little to those men. The answer lies in the
fact that as Ovid inherited the Pygmalion story from the Greeks,
Victor's guardians inherited from them the idea that man's nature
is whatever distinguishes him from the beasts. In Victor's case they

wanted some assurance that a creature who looked human but acted wild belonged to the human race.

One might think that Victor's membership in the human race would have been secure the first time he rode in a carriage pulled by horses. Then again, pet dogs can do as much. One might suppose that setting the table or eating with fork, knife, and spoon would have convinced his elders of his humanity. But as scholars have pointed out, the domestic "sphere" of society is generally perceived as being closer to nature than culture.[7] Given Itard's object of inducting Victor into human culture, the boy's adeptness at household tasks did not therefore count in his favor.

If nothing else, one might expect that Victor's displays of gratitude and his anticipations of Madame Guérin's needs would have won over his elders. The door of the nursery has been called the "gateway" of moral education, where habits and character traits that pave the way for rational morality are laid down.[8] In view of the fact that Victor's nursery was the forest, one can only marvel at his moral accomplishments. However, these scientists and philosophers were not the sort to be swayed by exhibitions of feeling or sentiment. They were men of the Enlightenment. To them, reason was the measure of man, and language the measure of reason.

Did not Victor employ reason when anticipating the needs of other people? Of course he did, and it also took intelligence for Victor to pocket all those sweets at the salon and run. But the kind of reason that Enlightenment thinkers attributed to man's nature was of a special sort.

"At five years old, mortals are not prepared to be citizens of the world, to be stimulated by abstract nouns, to soar above preference into impartiality," wrote George Eliot in *Daniel Deronda*, itself the story of an educational metamorphosis.[9] Yet to demonstrate his humanity, that cultural five-year-old named Victor would have had to stay at the salon dinner table and participate in the ongoing philosophical conversation that happened to be about the pros and cons of atheism and the beneficial properties of spiders (109). Or else he could have launched a new learned topic. Unless Victor were to offer up some fashionable meteorological theory the weather would not do, for this was no English tea party. But war or politics would have been quite acceptable subjects for discussion, as would the prevailing theory of mind.

Some have hypothesized that Victor might have made more linguistic progress if Itard had taught him sign language.[10] The proposal is not anachronistic. Sign language had been developed earlier in France by Abbé de l'Epée and by the 1770s it was being used to instruct those who could neither hear nor speak. When l'Epée died in 1789, his student Abbé de Sicard was named head of the new Institute for Deaf-Mutes, the very place where Itard would soon undertake his experiment with Victor. But even assuming that France's intelligentsia would have countenanced the substitution of signs for speech, the question remains of why it rated linguistic competence so much more highly than emotional well-being and moral maturity. That it did is incontrovertible.

In view of the philosophical leanings of the age, this value hierarchy is not surprising. In the seventeenth century the great French philosopher René Descartes had written:

> Language is in effect the sole sure sign of latent thought in the body; all men use it, even those who are dull or deranged, who are missing a tongue, or who lack the voice organs, but no animal can use it, and this is why it is permissible. (23)

And in the eighteenth century Étienne Bonnet de Condillac, whose philosophical treatises inspired the scientists and philosophers of Itard's day, maintained that language was the key to human thought. To be sure, he held that the sense organs are the source of knowledge. But after granting this much importance to the human body, he fixed his attention on the sensations and ideas deriving from them and on mental operations such as perceiving, remembering, and abstracting.

Indeed, the Cartesian thesis about language and humanity lives on into the twenty-first century. Commenting on a brain-damaged patient, the great twentieth-century Soviet neurologist A. R. Luria said: "Apart from being a means of communicating, language is fundamental to . . . thinking and behavior. . . . He [the patient] had lost what is distinctly human—the ability to use language."[11] As if in echo of the scholars who found Victor wanting, a linguist at the turn of the twenty-first century wrote, "Having a language, of course, is part of what it means to be human."[12]

For his part, Itard hoped that his experiment with Victor would confirm Condillac's thesis about language. He understood that there is more to human achievement than was dreamt of in Condillac's philosophy and knew that Victor had already learned some of that "more." Nevertheless, the fallacy at the heart of Enlightenment doctrine—namely, making language acquisition the essence of humanity—became the fatal flaw in his experimental design.

Might Victor have acquired language had the French government not ended Itard's experiment? Latter-day linguists put forward a "critical period hypothesis" for first language learning, in light of which Victor's chances of success would seem to have been slight. Thus, according to one highly regarded expert, "acquisition of a normal language is guaranteed for children up to the age of six, is steadily compromised from then until shortly after puberty, and is rare thereafter."[13] Whether Victor might have been an exception to this rule and at long last have succeeded in becoming fluent in French we will never know.

The problem of determining how fluent—if fluent at all—Victor might have become had Itard kept him on as a student is compounded by the fact that the experts hold to a very high standard of what counts as language acquisition. While in Itard's charge Victor learned to recognize many words, make known his wants, and even communicate them in writing. But whereas many people would say, "Well, then, Victor did acquire language after all," linguists and language acquisition specialists—in echo of the scientists and philosophers of Victor's time—are apt to insist that this is not enough. They are likely to maintain that to possess language, one must know its "deep structure" or "generative grammar"; that to have a smattering of vocabulary and a short list of two or three word sentences is no substitute. As one linguist has put it, a generative grammar "can crank out new arrangements of words. . . .With a few thousand nouns that can fill the subject slot and a few thousand verbs that can fill the predicate slot, one already has several million ways to open a sentence."[14]

The question is, where exactly in "the great chain of being" do these doubters put Victor? The great classifier Carolus Linnaeus named feral children a separate species and listed it among the quadrupeds.[15] A more broad-minded skeptic might instead put

Victor in a kind of limbo for newborns whose metamorphoses from nature are unsuccessful. Yet in light of all the cultural rules Victor learned and all the cultural practices he made his own, both judgments seem somewhat inflexible and unforgiving.

True, language is a characteristic of the human species. But art, tool making, agriculture, and self-awareness also characterize us.[16] Moreover, to specify a characteristic of the whole species is not to say that *every* human being possesses it or that this trait *has to be* possessed by an individual if he or she is to be considered human. Suppose a paralyzed man cannot make tools. Is he disqualified from the human race? Suppose a person lacks artistic talent or aesthetic sensibilities. Does he or she fall outside humanity? Surely not, and neither does a boy who can communicate with others and make his wants known in writing but lacks language in the experts' sense of the term.

Now it may be objected that art, tool making, and the rest are not on a par with language: they are *accidental* properties of the human species, whereas language usage is an *essential* property; indeed, the perfected form that the human species takes is that of rational language user. But what grounds are there for singling out one characteristic of the species rather than others and insisting that it be a property of each and every member of the species?

It has been suggested that were it not for language learning the transformation of newborns from "mere animals" to thinkers and intentional agents might seem mysterious; that a first language initiates humans into "a repository of tradition."[17] As it happens, Victor was initiated into the early nineteenth-century French traditions of walking, eating, dressing, table setting, attentiveness, and kindness without achieving the linguistic competence demanded by the experts. Moreover, in summing up his work with Victor, Itard wrote that "our savage" has

a knowledge of the conventional value of the symbols of thought and the power of applying this knowledge by naming objects, their qualities, and their actions. This has led to an extension of the pupil's relations with the people around him, to his ability to express his wants to them, to receive orders from them, and to effect a free and continual exchange of thoughts with them . . . in spite of his immoderate taste for the freedom of the open country and his indifference to most of the pleasures of social life, Victor is aware of the care taken

of him, susceptible to fondling and affection, sensitive to the pleasure of doing things well, ashamed of his mistakes, and repentant of
his outbursts. (160)

Victor may have lived a life of mental isolation. He would probably be minimally functional in twenty-first-century society.
Nonetheless, the deficits—and they are many—that stem from lan-
guagelessness in the technical sense do not take away the humanity of someone like Victor, who in other respects was transformed
from a creature of nature to an inhabitant of human culture.

A CURRICULUM MORE BASIC THAN THE 3Rs

Victor's case shatters the illusion that the walking and talking, the
eating and dressing, the manners, and the judgments of hot and
cold or far and near we call "second nature" spring up automatically. And so does the case of Genie. In the fall of 1970 a woman
walked into a Los Angeles county welfare office dragging behind
her a fifty-nine-pound teenager who from infancy had been kept in
isolation in a room of her father's home.[18] All those years Genie was
strapped down during the daytime to an infant potty seat. At night
she was placed in a sleeping bag that amounted to a straitjacket.

Genie was no Wild Child. She lived in a house with her parents,
not in the woods with the animals. Even in her isolation, she saw
people, heard them speak, and ate processed baby food. Yet her de-
ficiencies eerily matched Victor's when he came out of the woods
at more or less the same age. Her gait and posture were strange,
she could not chew solid food, she could barely swallow, she could
not focus her eyes beyond twelve feet, she could not distinguish
hot and cold, she was incontinent, and although she understood a
few words, she could only say "Stopit" and "Nomore." Upon her
admittance to Children's Hospital in Los Angeles, a doctor esti-
mated her motor skills to be at a two-year-old level and her emotional state to be that of "somber detachment" (42). Indeed, one observer noted that when in a room with other children, she did not
so much ignore or reject them as consider them no different from
the walls and furniture (60).

Genie's story, like Victor's, illustrates that what we adults
learned as very young children is far more basic than the school

studies we call our basics.[19] One of our culture's most deeply entrenched assumptions is that those things we call the basics of schooling are immutable givens. Thus, teachers are told that theirs is not to reason why, theirs is but to teach the 3Rs or die in the attempt. Yet it is not writ in stone that the 3Rs are the basics. The basics are not eternal, immutable givens from on high.

What makes one study rather than another a basic of education? What do reading, writing, and arithmetic have that cooking and driving, for example, do not? The answer cannot be that reading, writing, and arithmetic are essential for everyone to study whereas cooking and driving are not, for we call the 3Rs essential studies just because they are basic. Rather, the answer lies in the "generative power" of the 3Rs.

The philosophical notion of a basic action illuminates this metaphor of generative power. One opens a door by turning a knob, one pushes a stone by kicking it, one nods assent by moving one's head. Compare these acts with those one just does. One opens a door by turning the knob and one turns the knob by moving one's hand, but one just does move one's hand. One assents by nodding one's head but one just does move one's head. An act that requires no other act in doing it is called a "basic action" since it is the starting point or building block out of which other acts are formed.

Of course, from the standpoint of a general theory of human action, reading, writing, and arithmetic are not basic at all: one does not just do them; one does them by doing a variety of other actions. Furthermore, one must learn to do them. Yet from the standpoint of education the decision to call the 3Rs basic seems to make good sense. Education has to do with learning, and a great deal of learning—especially school learning—is done by reading, by writing, and by doing arithmetic. Moreover, the generative power of the 3Rs is not confined to learning. In contemporary society the 3Rs enter into our work and play, our jobs and recreation. We use them in our roles of consumer and parent, citizen and neighbor. One chooses one's candidates by keeping informed about the issues and one does this by reading the appropriate literature. At home one reads school announcements, sends email messages to the children's teachers, and pays the bills. At work one reads reports, checks out the appropriate websites, writes memoranda, and calculates the time spent on tasks.

The list of the everyday activities of living that are done by doing the 3Rs is endless. To be sure, for some acts of learning and living the 3Rs are irrelevant. Still, we call the 3Rs the basics of education because of their roles in preparing young people to be economically self-sufficient citizens in a democracy. We also take them to be fundamental because of the part they play in initiating our young into history, literature, science, mathematics, philosophy, and the arts—Culture with a capital "C."

Both Victor's case and Genie's demonstrate that these goals of education—achieving economic viability, becoming a good citizen, and acquiring high culture—make no sense for someone who has not already become a member of human culture. Their life stories suggest that achievement of even the limited goal of learning the 3Rs depends on a child's possessing the rudiments of culture with a small "c." For one of their main lessons is that this basic learning is imperiled when a child has not acquired the even more basic skills, knowledge, attitudes, values, and demeanors of human culture. In other words, just as the 3Rs have generative power vis-à-vis the acts of learning and living, the things a newborn learns during its metamorphosis from nature to culture have generative power vis-à-vis the 3Rs themselves.

It follows that if the 3Rs deserve to be called the basics of education, so much more so do those things that Victor had never dreamed of when he walked out of the woods, and that Genie could scarcely imagine either. And it also follows that if an education in the 3Rs is thought to be a requirement for all, so much more so should be the learning that comprises the first great metamorphosis from nature into culture. For if there is anything that everyone should learn it is the curriculum in walking, talking, and the rest that Victor was denied when he was abandoned in the woods.

IS THE FIRST GREAT METAMORPHOSIS AN EDUCATIONAL TRANSFORMATION?

A proviso is in order here. What a newborn learns as it is transformed from a creature of nature to a member of culture is educationally even more basic than the 3Rs *only if* the metamorphosis from nature to culture that we all undergo is an *educational* transformation.

As it happens, contemporary scholars and researchers are apt to deny that a first language is acquired through education. A belief widely subscribed to by those who study language is that the capacity to acquire a first language is innate.[20] No one holds that at birth a newborn can speak English or French or Japanese. Rather, the innate capacity that psychologists and linguists attribute to infants is to learn on a tacit or intuitive level the rules and patterns that constitute language's deep structure. In the eyes of some, one corollary of this "innateness hypothesis" is that education is superfluous: children acquire language without benefit of instruction, teaching, or any other form of education. Thus Noam Chomsky, the man who revolutionized the study of language, proposed that instead of saying that children "learn" language we should say that they "grow" it.[21]

Let us grant for the sake of argument that a young child does not require education in order to learn deep structure. Still, all those English or French or Japanese nouns and verbs that must accompany the knowledge of generative grammar if new phrases and sentences are to be cranked out do not just blossom as an infant develops. Furthermore, the cases of Victor and Genie leave no doubt that to learn or "grow" deep structure an infant needs to be in the right sort of environment. A newborn who has no access to English or French or Japanese will not learn to speak it. Indeed, a child who hears language from birth but whose mother or mother surrogate fails to bring the child into "a dialogue rich in communicative intent, in mutuality, and in the right sort of question" may not become a fluent speaker.[22]

The truth is that for most children first language acquisition does *seem* automatic. But the huge gap in the experience of both Victor and Genie—no mother or mother surrogate supplying the "right" kind of environment and behaving linguistically in the "right" ways—belies the hypothesis that a first language is acquired without benefit of some sort of education. To be sure, formal instruction is not required for children to be able to understand and communicate. But formal instruction is only one of the myriad forms that education takes. Socrates in dialogue with his friends in the market place, a baby sitter showing her charge how to navigate a jungle gym, a mother providing a rich oral environment for her child: these all qualify as educational episodes or events. And so does the familiar scene of a mother with her ten-month-old daughter on her lap who points to herself and says "Mommy," points to her three and a half year old and says "Catherine," and points to the baby and says "Olivia."

If one reduces "teaching" to telling or lecturing and defines "education" as a voluntary, intentional, self-aware activity, then much of the labor that is commonly performed by the mothers of newborns does not qualify as either one. And if one reduces learning to a strictly conscious, intentional activity, then a human infant can be said to acquire a first language without learning. But if "teaching" and "education" are defined more broadly as processes or activities that aim at—or else result in—learning outcomes; and if narrow definitions of learning are rejected: then mothers are reinstated as children's first teachers and educators and language acquisition is reinstated as an instance of learning.

To say this is not to deny that biological humans have an innate capacity to learn language. It is simply to say that if this innate capacity exists, language learning is not irrevocably removed from the educational realm. Some biological organisms, for example birds, have an innate capacity to fly. Humans do not. This capacity is not built into our "wiring" or neurological circuitry. On the other hand, humans can be said to have an innate capacity to learn to swim. But this does not preclude the great majority of us needing some sort of education—be it training, supervised practice, or what have you—if our innate capacity is to translate into swimming. Some organisms, most notably fish, have the innate capacity to swim—as opposed simply to the capacity to learn to swim—and that is enough: no instruction is necessary. But for most humans, the capacity to learn to swim amounts to wasted potential unless a suitable education is added. For humans, learning a first language is not like swimming is for fish—something that happens automatically—but like swimming is for us: something that we can do, given the right educational opportunities and treatment.

Actually, learning is so intimately bound up with education in the broad sense of the term that it is implausible to say that the innate capacity to learn language drives education out of the picture. For the very process of language learning makes one a participant in the educational process. True, education involves interaction between learner and environment. But so does language acquisition.

Language is, of course, only one of the traits or dispositions that enter into a newborn's first great metamorphosis. But the linguists and psychologists who deny that language acquisition is an educational affair would no doubt say the same thing about the traits of walking, distinguishing hot and cold, and all the rest. However, these claims also rely on overly narrow definitions of teaching and education.

In sum, just as one kernel of truth in the Pygmalion story is that education is open ended, another is that the first great metamorphosis human beings undergo does not just magically occur with the wave of a wand or by administering a potion and is not the product of development pure and simple. With marvelous art Pygmalion made a statue, says Ovid. As it is hard work to give human form to a piece of marble, it takes time and effort to teach a newborn manners and mores, time and effort to teach an infant to acquire a working vocabulary, time and effort to teach slightly older children to understand social duties and responsibilities. Victor's story bears this out. Making clear that the learning Victor achieved was the product of practice, patience, and directed effort on the parts of Itard and Mme. Guérin, it leaves not a shadow of a doubt that theirs was an educational achievement.

WHY IS THE FIRST GREAT METAMORPHOSIS SO OFTEN IGNORED?

Commenting on how deeply attached to the housekeeper Victor was, Itard described the boy's return home after an attempted escape back to the forest: "In the eyes of all the spectators he appeared less like a fugitive obliged to return to the supervision of his keeper than like an affectionate son who, of his own free will, comes and throws himself in the arms of the one who has given him life" (155). Victor's love for her, which was itself a function of the love Mme. Guérin bore him, seems to have made all the difference to his learning.

True, in Victor's case, both Itard's and Mme. Guérin's educational labors were Herculean. But in serving as the boy's surrogate mother in the old-fashioned sense of loving and taking care of him as a mother would, Mme. Guérin's share of the work reveals yet another kernel of truth in his story. Quite simply it is that the first great metamorphosis that each one of us undergoes is a relational affair involving not only hard work but also the circulation of love.

When it is recognized that the first great metamorphosis is an educational event, that it involves love as well as hard work, and that historically and cross-culturally most of the labor and the loving has been done by mothers and their surrogates, a mystery is solved. For what is so puzzling is not that newborns are transformed into members of culture. It is that although the first great metamorphosis is perhaps the most significant event in a person's life, theorists and philosophers of education have tended to neglect this phenomenon. Granted, it does not neatly conform to an incremental model. But there is more at stake here, for even if the change from being a creature of nature to a member of human culture did not take the form of a metamorphosis, the significance of the phenomenon would probably still be disregarded.

The key to the neglect lies in the fact that across history and across cultures, educating newborns has been thought of as women's special work and the kind of love whose object is the growth and development of children has also been considered the province of women. In a study of deaf people and language, twentieth-century neurologist Oliver Sacks wrote:

> A terrible power, it would seem, lies with the mother: to communicate with her child properly or not; to introduce probing questions such as "How?" "Why?" and "What if?" or replace them with a mindless monologue of "What's this?" "Do that"; to communicate a sense of logic and causality, or to leave everything at the dumb level of unaccountability; to introduce a vivid sense of place or time, or to refer only to the here and now; to introduce a "generalized reflection of reality," a conceptual world that will give coherence and meaning to life, and challenge the mind and emotions of the child, or to leave everything at the level of the ungeneralized, the unquestioned, at something almost below the animal level of the perceptual. Children, it would seem, cannot choose the world they will live in—the mental and emotion, any more than the physical world; they are dependent, in the beginning, on what they are introduced to by their mothers.[23]

One of the main contributions of the scholarship on women done in the last decades of the twentieth century was to demonstrate the extent to which women's lives, work, and accomplishments have been excluded from knowledge, textbooks, and the curriculum; or else have been grossly misrepresented. The disinterest in the first great metamorphosis and denial that it is an *educational* phenomenon is one more instance of that dismal finding.

The strange story of the distortion and neglect of home, family, and child rearing in the history of educational thought has already been told.[24] Rousseau is one of the few exceptions to the rule that the "world" of the private home—a world that his culture, like so many others, considered to be women's domain—held little interest for those in the past who cared about education. Indeed, although Rousseau did not call it a "metamorphosis," he described the contents of a newborn's education in some detail in Book I of *Emile*. Yet even though he understood that a child's education begins with the first great metamorphosis, he shied away from acknowledging that women have traditionally contributed the labor and love this transformation requires. Disregarding the facts, he made these tasks the domain of a male tutor.

One person in the history of educational thought who did not avoid the subjects of home, family, and the domestic affections was the Italian educator Maria Montessori. Indeed, she built domesticity and the kind of love whose object is the growth and development of children into her theory and her practice. It is perhaps no accident that she is also the person who studied the writings of Itard so closely and was so well acquainted with Victor's history that she wrote: "In the education of little children Itard's educative drama is repeated: we must prepare man, who is one among the living creatures and therefore belongs to nature, for social life."[25]

Just as there are two metamorphoses in the Pygmalion story, there are two kinds of love.[26] One kind is the romantic/sexual love that overtakes Ovid's sculptor once his statue of a woman is done. The other is the kind of love an artist feels for his materials and for the work of art in progress. Thinking of Victor's destiny and noticing that the poor of Rome had no time to spend with their children, Montessori developed an idea of school that gave pride of place to a form of love rather like Pygmalion's for his art. As he poured his energy into creating the most beautiful statues he possibly could, she gave teachers in her Casa dei Bambini responsibility for molding the best people they could. And just as Mme. Guérin's love for

Victor flowed to the boy and from him back to her, in Montessori's Casa dei Bambini the teachers' love for the children they taught also circulated.

Read Ovid's tale as an education story and it leaves no room for doubt about the overriding importance of the first great metamorphosis. Galatea could not possibly have become a flesh and blood woman if that block of ivory had not first been transformed into a statue. Furthermore, the statue of her would not have been so beautiful if Pygmalion had not cared so much about his art.

How ironic that the great majority of cultures have considered the form of education that is so essential to the continued existence of culture to be women's work, and women's work to be inferior to men's! When it is agreed that human culture itself has an overriding interest in the first great metamorphoses of newborns, the folly of putting just one portion of the population in charge of the curriculum of newborns is apparent. And how ironic, also, that education is so often considered an uninteresting, mundane activity!

Reporting on Itard's experiment with Victor, Montessori wrote: "Civilized life is made by renunciation of the life of nature; it is almost the snatching of a man from the lap of earth; it is like snatching the newborn child from its mother's breast; but it is also a new life."[27] Of the many kernels of truth contained in Victor's story, two stand out. One is that every viable member of human culture undergoes the life-shaping first great educational metamorphosis. The other is that this journey from nature into human culture is everyone's responsibility. And from these truths it follows that a culture's educational processes are as important as any processes on earth.

NOTES

1. Jean Paul Sartre, "Existentialism Is a Humanism," in *Existentialism from Dostoevsky to Sartre*, ed. Walter Kaufman (New York: Meridian Books, 1956), 295.

2. Sherry Ortner, "Is Female to Male as Nature Is to Culture?" in *Women, Culture, and Society*, ed. Michelle Zimbalist Rosaldo and Louise Lamphere (Palo Alto, CA: Stanford University Press, 1974), 77–78.

3. Clifford Geertz, *The Interpretation of Cultures* (New York: Basic Books, 1973), 49.

4. Jean-Jacques Rousseau, *Emile* (New York: Basic Books, 1973), 61.

5. The material on Victor is derived from Harlan Lane, *The Wild Boy of Aveyron* (Cambridge, MA: Harvard University Press, 1979). Page references are in parentheses in the text.

6. See, for example, Oliver Sacks, *Seeing Voices* (Berkeley: University of California Press, 1989), 60.

7. See, for example, Ortner, "Female to Male."

8. R. S. Peters, "Reason and Habit: The Paradox of Moral Education," in *Philosophy and Education*, ed. Israel Scheffler (Boston: Allyn and Bacon, 1966), 261.

9. George Eliot, *Daniel Deronda* (London: Penguin, 1986), 50.

10. See, e.g., Sacks, *Seeing Voices*, 11.

11. Susan Schaller, *A Man without Words* (New York: Summit Books, 1991), 88.

12. Steven Pinker, *The Language Instinct* (New York: Harper Perennial, 1995), 419.

13. Pinker, *The Language Instinct*, 298.

14. Steven Pinker, *The Blank Slate* (New York: Viking, 2002), 37.

15. Russ Rymer, *Genie* (New York: Harper Collins, 1993).

16. See, e.g., Jared Diamond, *Guns, Germs, and Steel* (New York: Norton, 1999), 139.

17. John McDowell, *Mind and World* (Cambridge, MA: Harvard University Press, 1994), 125–26.

18. The material on Genie is based on Rymer, *Genie*. Page references are in parentheses in the text.

19. The following analysis of the concept of the basics is based on Jane Roland Martin, *Changing the Educational Landscape* (New York: Routledge, 1994), chap. 10.

20. See, e.g., Pinker, *The Language Instinct*; Pinker, *The Blank Slate*.

21. Pinker, *The Blank Slate*, 33.

22. Sacks, *Seeing Voices*, 64.

23. Sacks, *Seeing Voices*, 65–66.

24. Jane Roland Martin, "The Love Gap in the Philosophy of Education Text," in *Teaching, Learning, and Loving*, ed. Daniel Liston and Jim Garrison (New York: Routledge Falmer, 2004), 21–34.

25. Maria Montessori, *The Montessori Method* (New York: Schocken, 1964), 153.

26. Perhaps even more. See, e.g., Ann Diller, "The Search for Wise Love in Education: What Can We Learn from the Brahmaviharas?" in Liston and Garrison, *Teaching, Learning, and Loving*, 169–84.

27. Montessori, *The Montessori Method*, 153.

3

Life as a
Chronology of Changes

THE CASE OF MALCOLM X

It has been said of Ovid's story of Pygmalion and Galatea: "Venus herself graced their marriage with her presence, but what happened after that we do not know."[1] Actually, we do know that nine months after her marriage to Pygmalion, Galatea gave birth to a daughter. What we do not know is what happened next. Did motherhood transform Galatea? When her daughter was grown, did Galatea undergo more metamorphoses?

The author of a study of her classmates at a New York City private school for girls twenty-five years after their graduation was repeatedly asked, "Didn't you find your classmates everything they used to be as girls—just more so?" No, she replied, "change has been the only constant, and metamorphosis has been all."[2] In a similar vein, Malcolm X said in his autobiography, "My life has been a chronology of changes."[3]

By his own reckoning Malcolm X underwent not one, not two, but four metamorphoses in his relatively short life, and this is without counting his first great transformation from a newborn to a member of culture. After having made that leap, the young Malcolm turned into a model schoolboy—so model, in fact, that in seventh grade he was elected president of his otherwise white junior high school class. Looking back, he said: "My grades were among the highest in the school. I was unique in my class, like a pink poodle. And I was proud; I'm not going to say I wasn't. In fact, by then, I didn't really have much feeling about being a Negro, because I was trying so hard, in every way I could, to be white" (31).

A few years passed and the "mascot"—this is Malcolm's term and the title of a chapter in the autobiography he wrote with the assistance of Alec Haley—was a Harlem hoodlum, thief, pimp, and drug addict. Recalling that period of his life he said, "I believe that it would be almost impossible to find anywhere in America a black man who has lived further down in the mud of human society than I have" (379). But the mud was no match for the person who was born Malcolm Little. Sent to prison, he pieced together a "home-made education" (171) that allowed him to emerge from the depths and become a leader of his people.

One might think that this many educational metamorphoses by the age of forty would be enough for anyone, but no. Shortly before his death, the man who had by then changed his name to Malcolm X traveled to Mecca and was once again transformed—this time from a separatist who believed that all white people are racist, into a citizen of the world.

Who played Pygmalion in this larger than life saga? For Malcolm Little there was no Henry Higgins or Jean-Marc-Gaspard Itard. His educators were his family, his school, his detention home, and his country's racial policies, practices, and prejudices. They were the "snooty-black neighborhood" (40) of Roxbury, the shoeshine stand where he first learned to hustle, and the railroad trains he rode to New York. They were Harlem in its various guises. And they were the Massachusetts Charlestown Prison, the Norfolk Prison Colony, the religion of Islam as interpreted by Elijah Muhammad, and Mecca.

Yet how accurate is it to call Malcolm's change from class president to hustler an "educational" metamorphosis? Malcolm's story challenges two common assumptions: that education is reducible to schooling and that education necessarily represents improvement. Malcolm knew firsthand that education does not take place only in school. In his autobiography he says wryly: "I finished the eighth grade in Mason, Michigan. My high school was the black ghetto of Roxbury, Massachusetts. My college was in the streets of Harlem, and my master's was taken in prison" (282). He also knew better than to equate education with progress. His own experience taught him that many of society's educational agents—in which category fall school, home, church, neighborhood and, indeed, all the other institutions of society—are profoundly miseducative.[4] And his life story demonstrates that educational transformations do not always add up to progress.

Science has frequently been described as a cumulative enterprise whose new discoveries build on old ones and whose most recent theories improve on those that came before. And it is often taken for granted that the education of an individual follows a similar straight-line trajectory. But although this comfortable vision of unending progress has been challenged in the case of science, many still take for granted that it holds true for education. Malcolm's life story disproves this assumption.

Malcolm's metamorphosis into a hustler was not brought about by a wave of a wand or the administration of a drug. Nor can it be chalked up to human development pure and simple. On the contrary, it was due to education in the broadest sense of that term— the sense that recognizes school as but one of education's agents, and that acknowledges that education can be either educative or *mis*educative.

Although the major part of Malcolm's miseducation took place in the streets and bars of Harlem, a crucial event in his transformation into a hustler occurred the day a junior high teacher told the model schoolboy, "You've got to be realistic about being a nigger. A lawyer—that's no realistic goal for a nigger. You need to think about something you *can* be. You're good with your hands—making things. Everybody admires your carpentry shop work. Why don't you plan on carpentry? People like you as a person—you'd get all kinds of work" (36). For all we know, the man may have thought he was being helpful. But regardless of his intentions, his words set in motion a transformation of the young boy's identity that can scarcely be considered an improvement on Malcolm's earlier transformation into a mascot. What follows from this radical change is that Malcolm was a different person, not a better person.

Referring later to his hustling self, Malcolm X said: "It is as though someone else I knew of lived by hustling and crime. I would be startled to catch myself thinking in a remote way of my earlier self as another person" (170). He could have said the same thing about his metamorphosis from mascot to hustler, for there was a radical disconnect between these two identities, too.

It has been said that after a scientific revolution, "scientists work in a different world."[5] As a scientist's shift of paradigm radically changes what he or she sees so that what were once familiar data now appear alien, Malcolm's transformation from hoodlum to leader so changed him that he found his earlier self unrecognizable. Although Shaw's Eliza makes no bones about the fact that she cannot go back to her flower basket, she remembers clearly the person she once was. Malcolm, on the other hand, was so changed that he could scarcely believe he was ever that hustler.

Malcolm's variation on Ovid's theme highlights the inherent unpredictability—even unruliness—of education. If looking backward it is hard to believe that an earlier self ever existed, how much harder it is to predict the nature of a future self! From model schoolboy to hustler. From hustler to leader of his people. No view of education as a series of small, incremental changes can capture the life-shaping changes Malcolm underwent.

IS MALCOLM X THE SAME
PERSON AS MALCOLM LITTLE?

Constructing a science fiction scenario, a philosopher asks if, after being teletransported to Mars, he is the same person. Splitting brains, a neurosurgeon cannot decide if the separate consciousnesses that have been produced belong to one person or if two selves inhabit the same body. The rest of us do not have to turn to fantasy or study the latest findings of neuroscience to wonder about personal identity. The cases of Malcolm, Victor, and Eliza strongly suggest that not one of us is the same person we once were and so does the case of the working-class heroine of Willy Russell's play, *Educating Rita*.

Says Rita about her husband: "I see him looking' at me sometimes, an' I know what he's thinking, I do y'know, he's wonderin' where the girl he married has gone to. He even brings me presents sometimes, hoping' that the presents'll make her come back. But she can't, because she's gone, an' I've taken her place."[6] Malcolm X in his turn told Haley that when his previous life's thinking pattern slid away from him in the Norfolk Prison Colony, he began to think of his former self as another person. These are no science fiction cases, nor are they written up in the annals of abnormal psychology. They are not the results of brain transplants, either. On the contrary, educational metamorphoses like the ones that Malcolm outlined in his autobiography and Russell portrayed in his play are the stuff of ordinary human life.

Acknowledging that everyone changes radically over time but insisting that it makes sense to say that someone is the same person today that he or she was yesterday, six months ago, or ten years past, philosophers pose what they call the problem of personal identity: What is it about a person whereby it can be truly said that he or she is the same person now as at an earlier time? The most important classical discussions of the problem of personal identity are those of English philosophers John Locke and David Hume, with Locke arguing that the criterion of identity is consciousness and Hume maintaining that there is no discernible bond or linkage that provides continuity over time. Although some followers of both Locke and Hume do exist today, few believe that the details of the solutions to the problem of personal identity presented by those men have withstood the test of time. For better or worse, however, the philosophical perplexity itself has passed the identity test: despite changes in its formulation over the centuries, radical disagreement over the criteria for personal identity persists into the present day.

Now a skeptic might say that no good can come from exploring the idea of educational metamorphosis before the general problem of personal identity is resolved. How can we know if Malcolm underwent whole person transformations if we do not know whether Malcolm the Harlem hustler and Malcolm the leader were the same person? If the skeptic were right and it were really necessary to solve the philosophical problem of identity before acknowledging the importance of educational metamorphoses, this discussion would have to be postponed, perhaps indefinitely. However, the deeply puzzling philosophical issue does not have to be resolved before we proceed, for the stories of Malcolm and Rita, Eliza and Victor represent crystal clear cases of whole person changes over time. Indeed, the question the skeptic needs to ask is not whether these metamorphoses meet one or another philosophical criterion of personal identity but how well the proffered criteria account for these great changes.[7]

But questions remain. At her very first meeting with Frank, her university tutor, Rita says that she has enrolled in the Open University in order to discover herself (12). One wonders why she uses the term *discover* as opposed to *construct* or *invent*. Does she think that, on the model of buried treasure, there is a self within her waiting to be unearthed? Is there such a thing? How does Rita know that she has a self quite different from the working-class wife/hairdresser self that her husband and friends know? And if she does have one, will she recognize it when she sees it?

Allusions like Rita's to a "true" or "real" or "authentic" self are common. Some people report strong feelings of a genuine self just waiting to emerge. Others compare a present inauthentic self to an authentic buried self that they know exists. From the age of three, wrote a woman who had undergone gender reassignment therapy, "the awareness that I was in the wrong body, living the wrong life, was never out of my conscious mind."[8] Furthermore, the idea of a self that will eventually be revealed to its "owner" appears to solve the problem of personal identity over time. If an underlying, unseen, enduring self exists in each person, then there is good reason to judge an individual to be the same person now as in the past, even though he or she has changed radically during that interval.

The idea of a true or real self also has persuasive value. What better way is there to convince a boy who just got into a fight with a friend to change his behavior than to tell him that you know there is a better self inside him that is just waiting to emerge? In addition, the fact that when an educational metamorphosis occurs some of a person's old characteristics will likely carry over into the new self lends credence to the idea of an enduring self.

Consider Malcolm's several transformations. There is no reason to suppose that every trait he displayed as a schoolboy was erased when he became a hustler, or even that every characteristic of Malcolm the hustler was eradicated when he became a leader. On the contrary, throughout his life and across his several metamorphoses Malcolm seems to have been a highly intelligent, enterprising, and magnetic person. True, like everything else these constants in his character changed and developed over time. Nonetheless, several of Malcolm's personal traits or characteristics appear to have survived his several educational metamorphoses in broad outline even if not in every specific. In this respect his life story is not unique. Just as Eliza the flower girl has qualities that survive her transformation into a lady, the boy we meet in the next chapter remains a quick learner and an excellent athlete after his metamorphosis from an Inuit into an American boy.

Yet no matter how tempting it is to call those traits that persist across a person's educational metamorphoses his or her "true" or "authentic" self, numerous problems attach to this idea. First, there is the issue of how one knows that a buried self exists. When a person undergoes several metamorphoses, there is also the question of which self represents the "true" or "real" self. Is Malcolm's model schoolboy self truer or more real than his hustling self? Is his leader of black people self a more or less genuine self than the world citizen self that was revealed shortly before his assassination? And finally, there is the question of what sort of entity a self is that exists even when an individual is unaware of it and other people see no signs of it. It is not an ordinary physical object. But then, what is it? Where, moreover, did it come from and what possible justification is there for assuming that it is enduring?

At present, definitive answers to questions like these are not available. Thankfully, so long as the idea of educational metamorphoses is comprehensible independently of the assumption that there is an underlying, unseen, enduring self, they are not required. Let us, therefore, acknowledge the reality of first and third person perceptions and descriptions of this kind of self and withhold judgment about the actual existence of such an entity.

Let it be noted that to adopt a neutral stance regarding the existence of an underlying, unseen, enduring self is not to ban talk of preexisting potentialities. Just as linguists and psychologists say that a human newborn has the capacity or potential to learn a language, many a pugnacious boy can be said to have the capacity or potentiality to be nonviolent. But this does not mean that there is a nonviolent self inside him just waiting to emerge. Rather, it is to say that under the right conditions, he could learn to be nonviolent in his interactions with his peers. Similarly, when Malcolm says about his prison awakening, "the ability to read awoke inside me some long dormant craving to be mentally alive" (179), we need not conclude that he all along possessed a submerged, mentally alive self. His words may be understood to mean that under the right conditions—ones that in fact occurred—he could become a mentally alive person.

Suppose for the sake of argument, however, that the hypothesis of an underlying self is true. Even then it does not follow that a person who undergoes an educational metamorphosis is the sole authority regarding the transformational experience or even the best one. In the first place, it is unlikely in the extreme that young children are the best judges of whether their own first great metamorphosis has occurred. A three-, four-, or five-year-old does not remember all the changes she has undergone since birth, let alone being a newborn. Furthermore, even knowledgeable adults can be mistaken about—or else intentionally give a false impression of—their educational histories.

By virtue of wishful thinking, a woman or man may feel like a different person without actually having become one. Or an individual may think a radical change has occurred although it has not, because she or he badly wants it to be so or else misremembers the self that has supposedly been left behind. Then again, a person may have ulterior purposes such as the avoidance of punishment for claiming to have undergone an educational metamorphosis. For these reasons and more it is a mistake to conclude that a person's claim to having undergone an educational metamorphosis is irrefutable.

Does this mean that a third party's judgment of whether an educational metamorphosis has taken place will necessarily be correct? Eliza says she cannot go home again, but someone more versed in pretense than she might return as a lady to Covent Garden and playact at being a flower girl so convincingly that her old friends believe her. On visits to his parents a dutiful son who has long since been transformed by his higher education might similarly feign that he is the same person he used to be so as to avoid their disapproval of his new pursuits or keep them from feeling that he has deserted them. And, on the other hand, the perpetrator of a crime may lay claim to a whole person metamorphosis he has never experienced in order to escape sentencing.

If both first- and third-person claims regarding the occurrence of a successful educational metamorphosis are open to challenge, how are we to decide if one has occurred? In order to avoid hypocrisy and self-deception, we must determine not simply how a person thinks but also how that individual behaves, sees him or herself, and lives in the world. Indeed, to insure that a whole person change has in fact occurred, we must determine all this for both the initial and the end state of the metamorphosis. Because the phenomena in question are educational, we must in addition ascertain that the transformation is due to learning and not simply to drugs or surgery or the wave of a wand.

In light of these complications, judgments about the success, or lack thereof, of educational metamorphoses may seem daunting. Yet despite their complexity they do not differ significantly from judgments about whether any other kind of learning has taken place. When a schoolchild says, "I know the dates of the U.S. Civil War," does this mean that learning has just now occurred? Perhaps the child already knew the dates. Or perhaps the child is indulging in wishful thinking or is engaged in self-delusion. Suppose the child answers a question about the dates correctly. Can a teacher or some other third party say with absolute certainty that the child has just now learned the dates? The child might have known them for years. Or else the girl or boy might have accidentally hit on the right answer to the test question. For a third party to decide if incremental change has occurred, he or she must look at a wide range of behaviors both past and present, and must also be willing to alter the judgment in light of new evidence. The case is no different for educational metamorphoses.

THE IDEA OF MULTIPLE EDUCATIONAL AGENCY

Malcolm cited prison, Harlem, Islam as the agents that brought about his metamorphoses. Someone else might list home, family, church, Girl Scouts as the agents of theirs. It is common knowledge that education is everywhere. No one raises an eyebrow when religious leaders present themselves as educators, museums house education departments, or television networks label some programs "educational." No one thinks that school and university teachers are the only educators in our midst. Yet articles in the education section of newspapers and magazines are about schools and universities. Commissioners of education make schools their domain. Scholars say that educational levels have risen when what they really mean is that there has been an increase in years of school attendance.

Education has not always been equated with schooling. Consider the colonial period in U.S. history. The family was the main agent of education in the forming of U.S. society, and whatever it did not accomplish, the local community and the church undertook.[9] Schools existed but they played a relatively small role. Indeed, although Thomas Jefferson was a firm advocate of schooling, he never thought of school as the chief educational influence on the young.[10] In Jefferson's eyes, the press and participation in politics were the main educational agencies. Even when a system of free, universal, public schooling was under construction in the mid-nineteenth century, most people took school to be a minor part of education. The generation that instituted "the common school" is also the one that established public libraries, lyceums, mechanics' institutes, agricultural societies, penny newspapers. And the next generation introduced still more agencies, among them the social settlement.

The unique pattern of *multiple educational agency* that characterized an earlier historical period cannot be recovered, but this does not justify giving school a monopoly over education.[11] Important as school has become, it is still only one of society's educational agents. Home is another. Church, neighborhood, police and fire departments, museums, historical societies, libraries, and archives; zoos, parks, playgrounds, aquariums, and arboretums; symphony orchestras, record clubs, recording companies, ballet troops, and opera houses; banks, businesses, and the stock market; newspapers, magazines, book clubs, book stores, publishing houses; sports organizations, billboards, government agencies, the military establishment, nonprofit organizations, and environmental groups; TV, the Internet, and the media in all its multitudinous forms: these and the myriad other institutions of society also educate young and old.

The idea that educational agency takes multiple forms brings to mind the twentieth-century French philosopher Michel Foucault's analysis of power. Foucault pointed out that we tend to imagine power as centralized: as coming from above and as being located in the hands of a sovereign. In fact, he said, power operates in all the nooks and crannies of society and gains "access to individuals themselves, to their bodies, their gestures, their daily actions."[12] On this view, power is located in schools, prisons, the confessional; in the psychiatric profession's diagnostic categories of mental illness, the medical profession's standards of obesity, a corporation's decision to play music while a caller is on hold, a magazine's tips on dieting, a department store's display of cosmetics.

Once the concept of power is decentralized, the list of its sites and sources becomes endless. When the equation between education and schooling is rejected and education is in its turn decentralized, the list of educational agents is also unending. Foucault did not deny that the state is important. He simply wanted the analysis of power to extend beyond it. And, as one interpreter has put it, he wanted it to begin "from the ground up, at the level of tiny local events."[13] In like-minded fashion, the idea of educational metamorphoses acknowledges school's importance while extending the analysis of educational agency well beyond school. It also recognizes that educational agency is at work from the ground up. Where, for example, does the subliminal message that war is natural whereas peace is hopelessly unrealistic come from? A child receives it in the sandbox and on the playground before being fed it by films, television, electronic games, newspapers, magazines, and political parties.

Rousseau said in *Emile* that education comes to us "from nature or from men or from things."[14] Two centuries later social critic Ivan Illich called things, models, peers, and elders the resources a child needs for "real learning."[15] Both men were correct in saying that learning derives from people and things, yet no good can come from oversimplifying educational agency. One lesson Malcolm's story teaches is that in real life things and people are not encountered in the abstract "as such." Rather, they come embedded in some institutional context.

Compare a college student reading W. E. B. Dubois's *The Souls of Black Folk* for a course in African-American studies with Malcolm's reading this book in prison. Said Malcolm: "My homemade education gave me, with every additional book that I read, a little bit more sensitivity to the deafness, dumbness, and blindness that was afflicting the black race in America" (179). Furthermore, a given person or thing can move, as it were, from one context to another: a Mayan vase from an archeological site to a museum; a lullaby from a mother's lips to a concert stage. And with changes in context come great changes in what messages are transmitted and learned. For these reasons, the "designated educational agents" in this discussion of educational metamorphoses are institutions rather than "free-floating" individuals, where the term *institution* is defined broadly enough to include associations, groups, cultural settings, and the like.

Chapter 3

THE REALITY OF HIDDEN CURRICULA

A skeptic may wonder if the subliminal messages that institutions send really add up to education. Here again Foucault's analysis of power is helpful. Rejecting analyses that give pride of place to intention, he urged that the analysis of power "should not concern itself with power at the level of conscious intention or decision."[16] What is needed, he said, "is a study of power in its external visage, at the point where it is in direct and immediate relationship with that which we can provisionally call its object, its target, its field of application, there—that is to say—where it installs itself and produces its real effects."[17]

In the case of education it would be a grave mistake to ignore the level of conscious intention or decision. On the other hand, to build intentionality and awareness of what one is doing into the definition of education is to lose sight of a vast amount of learning that actually takes place. A manufacturer who has no interest in education and whose sole intention is to make a profit markets a game where the object is an escalating body count. While the company rakes in a profit, the players of the game receive messages about the acceptability of violence and the cheapness of life. The producers of a television talk show seek to entertain not educate their viewers. Yet even as the laughter registers, audience members are at the very least acquiring information—or possibly misinformation—and quite possibly a whole range of attitudes and values as well.

Rejecting the false equation between education and schooling and roundly condemning school's hidden curriculum, Illich called for the "deschooling" of society. Schools make people dependent on school without really educating them, he said. Send students into the world at large: that is where they can get a genuine education. As it was Shaw's genius to read Ovid's Pygmalion poem as an education story, it was Illich's to make the idea of multiple educational agency a central element of his philosophy, although he did not call it this. But just as Shaw let one crucial element of Ovid's myth, namely the transformation of newborns, drop out of the picture, in *Deschooling Society* Illich to all intents and purposes allowed the hidden curricula of nonschool educational agents to go unseen.

School and all the other institutions of society have both an overt or explicit curriculum and a hidden curriculum.[18] To ignore what is unintentionally taught and learned both outside and in school is to arrive, at best, at a truncated vision of education—one that sheds little light on cases like Malcolm's. When Malcolm's teacher told him that being a lawyer was not a realistic goal for a nigger, he had no idea of the radical changes in the boy his words would inspire. Nor did Chinese immigrant Elaine Mar's first-grade classmates in Denver, Colorado, know how their words would affect her. On the playground the older children joked that her hair and skin were being pulled too tight. "The children's voices crawled inside me and took residence. I wished I weren't so pathetic. I hated myself almost as much as they did."[19]

To build voluntariness, intentionality, and self-awareness into the very concept of educational agency is to cast hidden curricula outside education's realm. One of the worst byproducts of a centralized conception of educational agency is that no institution other than school can, in good logic, be charged with miseducating the populace. Yet in daily bombarding young people with unwholesome, antisocial models of living and in making these appear fatally attractive, the print and electronic media are guilty of doing precisely this.

THE LIMITS OF AN ACADEMIC EDUCATION

Illich maintained that the hidden curriculum of schooling teaches us to confuse grade advancement with education and a diploma with competence. Malcolm learned this lesson well even though he left school after eighth grade. Reflecting on his prison experience, he told Haley: "I don't think anybody ever got more out of going to prison than I did. In fact, prison enabled me to study far more intensively than I would have if my life had gone differently and I had attended some college" (180). Yet he also said: "My greatest lack has been, I believe, that I don't have the kind of academic education I wish I had been able to get" (379). And he added: "I would not be one bit ashamed to go back into any New York City public school and start where I left off at the ninth grade, and go through a degree. Because I don't begin to be academically equipped for so many of my interests" (380).

There is no way of telling what kind of person Malcolm would have been had he received the formal education that in his final days he said he wanted. He himself said:

> I've often thought that if Mr. Ostrowski had encouraged me to become a lawyer, I would today probably be among some city's professional black bourgeoisie, sipping cocktails and palming myself off as a community spokesman for and leader of the suffering black masses, while my primary concern would be to grab a few more crumbs from the groaning board of the two-faced whites with whom they're begging to integrate. (38)

No one can know if this scenario would have come to pass. It is safe to say, however, that if Malcolm had received the academic education whose lack he so regretted, he might well have turned into a very different person from the man he eventually became.

Suppose that Mr. Ostrowski had encouraged Malcolm and that the boy had graduated from high school and attended college. He would have learned to speak and write the language of the educated class instead of having to teach himself the 3Rs while in prison. He told Haley that in simple written English, "I not only wasn't articulate, I wasn't even functional" (171). When reading books in Charlestown Prison, Malcolm skipped the words "that might as well have been in Chinese" and he was still "going through only book-reading motions" when he was transferred to Norfolk (171). Once he arrived at the more open facility, he requested and was given a dictionary, pencils, and tablets.

> I spent two days just riffling uncertainly through the dictionary's pages. I'd never realized so many words existed! I didn't know *which*

words I needed to learn. Finally, just to start some kind of action, I began copying.

In my slow, painstaking, ragged handwriting, I copied into my tablet everything printed on that first page, down to the punctuation marks.

I believe it took me a day. Then, aloud, I read back, to myself, everything I'd written on the tablet. Over and over, aloud, to myself, I read my own handwriting.

I woke up the next morning, thinking about those words— immensely proud to realize that not only had I written so much at one time, but I'd written words that I never knew were in the world. Moreover, with a little effort, I also could remember what many of these words meant. . . .

I was so fascinated that I went on—copied the dictionary's next page. And the same experience came when I studied that. With every succeeding page, I also learned of people and places and events from history. Actually the dictionary is like a miniature encyclopedia. Finally, the dictionary's A section had filled a whole tablet—and I went on into the B's. That was the way I started copying what eventually became the entire dictionary. . . .

I suppose it was inevitable that as my word-base broadened, I could for the first time pick up a book and read and now begin to understand what the book was saying. (172)

With an academic education in hand Malcolm would have been saved this struggle. But mastery of the language of the educated class would not have enabled him to communicate with many of the people he ultimately reached. He told Haley: "I knew that the ghetto people knew that I never left the ghetto in spirit, and I never left it physically any more than I had to. I had a ghetto instinct; for instance, I could feel if tension was beyond normal in a ghetto audience. And I could speak and understand the ghetto's language" (310). Observing Malcolm's daily rounds in Harlem, Haley wrote, "Malcolm X loved it. And they loved him . . . the man had charisma, and he had *power*" (403).

Had Malcolm gone to college he might have read widely, but the books he studied would not have been the same ones he read in prison. On his own, he constructed a Black—or African-American— studies curriculum for himself before the field was ever invented. For a start Malcolm pored over an encyclopedia, *Wonders of the World*, Will Durant's *Story of Civilization*, H. G. Wells's *Outline of*

History, W. E. B. Dubois's *Souls of Black Folk,* and Carter G. Wood-
son's *Negro History.* Then he read Gregor Mendel's *Findings in Ge-
netics* and book after book about slavery. Next he turned to
Herodotus and Gandhi, and studied volumes showing "how the
white man had brought about the world's black, brown, red and
yellow peoples every variety of the sufferings of exploitation" (176).
After digesting everything he possibly could about world history
and politics, he turned to philosophy and "tried to touch all the
landmarks of philosophical development" (179), among them
Schopenhauer, Kant, Nietzsche, and Spinoza. And of course he read
Shakespeare and Milton.

An academic education might in addition have developed Malcolm's reasoning ability and his analytical and critical powers. It is
unlikely, however, that college would have had the effect that
prison did: "It was right there in prison," Malcolm told Haley, "that
I made up my mind to devote the rest of my life to telling the white
man about himself" (184–85).

Consider what happens to Willy Russell's Rita when she enrolls
in the Open University. Once she begins to read, write, and talk
about English literature—once she becomes so absorbed in the subject she can scarcely think about anything else—her identity change
is under way. Before long, where she once saw poems she could not
understand, books too immoral to read, and BBC programs too
boring to watch, she sees "high" culture. Where she once talked
and walked and dressed like a working-class hairdresser, she looks
and sounds and behaves like a new person—an educated woman.

Rita is convinced that as an educated person she will lead a better life:

> I've tried to explain it to me husband but between you an' me I think
> he's thick. No, he's not thick, he's blind, he doesn't want to see. You
> know if I'm readin', or watchin' somethin' different on the telly he
> gets dead narked. . . . I tried to explain that I wanted a better way of
> livin' me life. And he listened to me. But he didn't understand be-
> cause when I'd finished he said he agreed with me and that we
> should start savin' the money to move off our estate an' get a house
> out in Formby. (12)

Her belief that art and literature, opera and theater are higher pursuits than singing songs learned from a jukebox is a staple of West-

ern thought. One of its most famous formulations is to be found in *Utilitarianism*, John Stuart Mill's great treatise on ethics. There Mill insisted that some pleasures—most notably intellectual ones—have higher value than others.

In a famous passage Mill wrote:

> It is better to be a human being dissatisfied than a pig satisfied; better to be Socrates dissatisfied than a fool satisfied. And if the fool, or the pig, are of a different opinion, it is because they only know their own side of the question. The other party to the comparison knows both sides.[20]

Is there any doubt that Rita would cast her former self as the fool and her future one as a human being; or, for that matter, Denny as the pig and Frank as Socrates?

Paradoxically, the character with experience of both Mill's higher and lower pleasures is not sanguine about Rita's future. When Frank meets Rita he tells her that she is the first breath of fresh air that has been in his office for years (11). Some weeks later he says that her recent paper on *Macbeth* is "a totally honest, passionate account of your reaction to a play. It's an unashamedly emotional statement" (47). When Rita asks if it is sentimental—something he has told her she must never be if she wants to pass her exams—he replies with embarrassment that it is almost moving. He also assures her that in terms of what she wants him to teach her it is worthless. When Rita expresses the wish to write essays like the ones in the pile on his desk, he protests: "If you're going to write this sort of thing . . . you're going to have to suppress, perhaps even abandon your uniqueness" (48).

Like Eliza at Wimpole Street and Malcolm in prison, Rita undergoes a whole person transformation. In act one she says: "Sometimes I wonder if I'll ever understand any of it. It's like startin' all over again, y' know with a different language" (36). By play's end she is not merely fluent in the language of literary criticism: her speech approximates that of an educated person. When Rita first meets Frank she promises him that when she passes her first examination, "I'll get a proper dress, the sort of dress you'd only see on an educated woman" (18). In the last act she says: "I've got a room full of books. I know what clothes to wear, what wine to buy, what plays to see, what papers and books to read" (68).

Frank balks not so much at Rita's learning to use her "higher" faculties and experience the "higher" pleasures as at what she sacrifices in the process. As if in echo of the philosophers and scientists who determined Victor's fate, he tells her at their second meeting that passing her exams will require the suppression of feeling and emotion. "You must remember that criticism is purely objective," he says. "It should be approached almost as a science. It must be supported by reference to established literary critique. Criticism is never subjective and should not be confused with partisan interpretation. In criticism sentiment has no place" (18).

To appreciate fully the authors she reads Rita must also stop worrying about the problems of the world. When Frank first asks her what she thinks of E. M. Forster's *Howard's End*, she calls it "crap." "When he wrote that book," says Rita, "the conditions of the poor in this country were appalling. An' he's sayin' he couldn't care less." Frank reprimands her for being sentimental: "You stopped reading the book because you wanted Forster to concern himself with the poor. Literature can ignore the poor" (19). "Well, it's immoral," she replies. "Amoral," says Frank.

By the end of the play Rita has learned this lesson well. Bringing her newly developed intellectual capacities to bear on the problem of poverty that she once felt so keenly is not on her agenda. When Frank asks her what she is going to do now that she has passed her exam she says, "I dunno. I might go to France. I might go to me mother's. I might even have a baby. I dunno. I'll make a decision, I'll choose. I dunno" (72–73).

In fairness to Mill it must be said that he would not have condoned the university's siphoning off of reason from feelings and emotions. Nor would he have approved the divorce of reason from the impulse to make the world a better place. In a section of his *Autobiography* entitled "A Crisis in My Mental History," Mill wrote that the habit of analysis "has a tendency to wear away the feelings" and that the analytic habits that had constituted the core of his own education are "but a perpetual worm at the root both of the passions and the virtues."[21] He did not deny the many values of an analytic frame of mind. But in looking back on the ultrarigorous academic education designed for him by his psychologist father and his father's friend, philosopher Jeremy Bentham, he could see that it had failed to create in him sympathy with human beings and the feelings that make the good of others one's source of happiness. And so, the cultivation of feelings became "one of the cardinal points of my ethical and philosophical creed."[22]

Still, Rita's experience conforms to the culture's idea of an academic education. Indeed, one great irony of the education Western culture has historically called "liberal" is that it is neither broad nor generous. Another irony is that the kind of education Malcolm X regretted not having had might well have turned him into a spectator of events instead of the active participant in life that he became.

In *Up from Slavery*, Booker T. Washington, a nineteenth-century leader of African Americans, reported that while he was a student at Hampton Institute in Virginia he organized a debating society so that he and the other students could use their free time practicing public speaking.[23] Three-quarters of a century later Malcolm told of joining the prison debating club. "My reading had my mind like steam under pressure. Some way I had to start telling the white man about himself to his face. I decided I could do this by putting my name down to debate" (184). Did Homer Exist? Compulsory Military Training—or None? Should Babies Be Fed Milk? Shakespeare's True Identity? Malcolm learned how to turn each and every topic to his advantage:

> Standing up and speaking before an audience was a thing that throughout my previous life never would have crossed my mind. Out there in the streets, hustling, pushing dope, and robbing, I could have had the dreams from a pound of hashish and I'd never had dreamed anything so wild as that one day I would speak in coliseums and arenas, at the greatest American universities, and on radio and television programs, not to mention speaking all over Egypt and Africa and in England.
>
> But I will tell you that right there, in the prison, debating, speaking to a crowd, was as exhilarating to me as the discovery of knowledge through reading had been. Standing up there, the faces looking at me, the things in my head coming out of my mouth, while my brain searched for the next best thing to follow what I was saying, and if I could sway them to my side by handling it right, then I had won the debate—once my feet got wet, I was gone on debating. (184)

Getting inside the skin of one of her heroines, British novelist Margaret Drabble said: "But the fact that she could no longer remember the self that had married Christopher, nor the self that had signed that cheque, did not mean that they had not been necessary."[24] The great irony of Malcolm's transformation from mascot into hustler is that it eventually landed him in a place where he had time enough to read *and* think about the sufferings and the exploitation of black people around the world: time he might not have had, if he had gone to college and received there a traditional academic education. For him, prison was also the place where he learned to say what was on his mind.

The great insight to be gleaned from Malcolm's variation on Ovid's Pygmalion theme is that human life is indeed a chronology of change. Granted, few lives are as dramatic as Malcolm's and few people experience such radical whole person changes in their lifetimes as he did. Yet just as Victor's case has meaning for the plight of all newborns, so Malcolm's can be generalized.

A teenage boy inherits his brother's job of trash collector for a small building. Will he, following his brother's lead, do his work and leave the premises as quickly as he can? Or will he hang around, befriend the college graduates in one of the apartments, enlist their help in doing his homework, become their protégé, and eventually be the proud recipient of a college diploma and an utterly different person? A woman with a grown daughter gets divorced after a long marriage. Will she withdraw into herself and become an embittered or perhaps a self-abnegating person or will she, like the writer Frances Mayes, buy a house in Tuscany and invent a new future?[25] Either way she will become a brand new individual. An eighteen-year-old college freshman is beaten and raped. "My life was over; my life had just begun," she wrote in a memoir of the cataclysmic event.[26]

The details of every life and every metamorphosis will be different. Nevertheless, just as Victor's story demonstrates that practically every single one of us undergoes an educational metamorphosis from being a creature of nature to an inhabitant of human culture, Malcolm's teaches that almost every human life takes the form of a series or succession of educational metamorphoses.

In view of the many different kinds of educational metamorphoses there are, this is not surprising. Events in the life cycle, personal traumas, professional training, political movements, immigration from one country to another, changes in one's class position: representing occasions for whole person transformations, these and more support the conclusion that every life resembles Malcolm's in being a chronology of change. But that is not all. If one hypothesis to be drawn from Malcolm's case is that after a bit of reflection almost everyone could supply at least a partial list of his or her own identity transformations, another hypothesis is that for each one of us there may be at least one more educational metamorphosis in the offing.

NOTES

1. Edith Hamilton, *Mythology* (New York: New American Library, 1953), 111.
2. Elizabeth Fishel, *Reunion* (New York: Random House, 2000), 280–81.
3. Malcolm X. *The Autobiography of Malcolm X* (New York: Grove Press, 1966), 330. Page references are in parentheses in the text.
4. For an extended discussion of miseducative institutions see Jane Roland Martin, *Cultural Miseducation* (New York: Teachers College Press, 2002).
5. Thomas S. Kuhn, *The Structure of Scientific Revolutions* (Chicago: University of Chicago Press, 1970, 2nd ed.), 135.
6. Willy Russell, *Educating Rita* (Essex: Longman Group, 1985,) 33. Page references are in parentheses in the text.
7. In other words, the assumption that solutions to the problem of personal identity are in some important sense prior to specific instances of educational metamorphosis gets things backwards. To establish the existence of educational metamorphoses it is not necessary that there be an agreed upon criterion of personal identity. Rather, the adequacy of solutions to the personal identity problem depends, at least in part, on how well they can account for this type of change over time. Instead of viewing solutions to the problem of personal identity as providing formulas against which to test the validity of individual educational metamorphoses, we need to recognize that these phenomena represent data against which solutions to the problem of identity must be tested.
8. Jennifer Finney Boylan, *She's Not There* (New York: Broadway Books, 2003), 19.
9. Bernard Bailyn, *Education in the Forming of American Society* (New York: Viking, 1960).
10. Lawrence Cremin, *The Genius of American Education* (New York: Vintage, 1965).

11. For more on the false equation between education and schooling and the idea of multiple educational agency, see Martin, *Cultural Miseducation.*

12. Michel Foucault, *Power/Knowledge: Selected Interviews and Other Writings 1972–1977* (New York: Pantheon, 1980), 151–52.

13. Ian Hacking, "The Archeology of Foucault," in *Foucault: A Critical Reader,* ed. D. C. Hoy (Oxford: Blackwell, 1986), 28.

14. Jean-Jacques Rousseau, *Emile* (New York: Basic Books, 1979), 38.

15. Ivan Illich, *Deschooling Society* (New York: Harper & Row, 1972), 109.

16. Foucault, *Power/Knowledge,* 97.

17. Foucault, *Power/Knowledge,* 97.

18. I do not mean to suggest that Illich did not know this. Nonetheless, in proposing in *Deschooling Society* that in lieu of schools there could be such things as tool shops, libraries, laboratories, gaming rooms, photo labs, storefront learning centers, film clubs, museum outlets, biology stores, and commercial television he neglected to say that these might have hidden curricula of their own, not all of which would necessarily be benign.

19. M. Elaine Mar, *Paper Daughter* (New York: Perennial, 1999), 72.

20. John Stuart Mill, *Utilitarianism, On Liberty, Essay on Bentham* (New York: New American Library, 1962), 260.

21. John Stuart Mill, *Autobiography* (Oxford: Oxford University Press, 1952), 116, 117.

22. John Stuart Mill, *Autobiography,* 122.

23. Booker T. Washington, *Up from Slavery,* in *Three Negro Classics* (New York: Avon Books, 1965), 65.

24. Margaret Drabble, *The Needle's Eye* (New York: Alfred A. Knopf, 1972), 85.

25. Frances Mayes, *Under the Tuscan Sun* (New York: Broadway Books, 1997).

26. Alice Sebold, *Lucky* (New York: Scribner, 1999), 41.

4

Educational Metamorphoses as Culture Crossings

THE CASE OF MINIK

Almost exactly one century after Victor came out of the forest, a seven-year-old boy from northwestern Greenland named Minik walked into Western civilization.[1] In many respects their sagas are alike. Minik also became an instant celebrity. He too was made an object of scientific curiosity. And as if determined to confirm the old adage that history repeats itself, the scientific community abandoned him as quickly as it had deserted Victor. Yet Minik was no Wild Child.

Before Victor emerged from the woods he had learned enough to survive there, but he had not yet made that great leap from nature to human culture. In Rousseau's words, Victor had not yet learned "to feel the hotness, the coldness, the hardness, the softness, the heaviness, the lightness, of bodies, and to judge their size, their shape, and all their sensible qualities."[2] Nor did he know how to judge distances and feel changes of place, let alone to walk, talk, and dress himself.

When Minik and his father sailed to New York City with Arctic explorer Robert Peary, he could do much more than walk and talk. Before boarding Peary's ship, Minik heard a scientist in the party promise a jackknife to the first child who could deliver him an owl.

With a small bow and arrow he collected the prize. After he learned
English, Minik told reporters:

> Once my father had a very good dog. One day it fell into a big—very
> big—crack in the ice. Then my father say to me that I go down after
> the dog. My father tie a rope around my shoulders, and then they let
> me down into the big crack in the ice. I tie the rope around the dog,
> and the men pull us both up, so we have saved the dog. (46)

Minik may, of course, have been exaggerating his prowess. But
according to Kenn Harper, the historian who reconstructed Minik's
life, this was not an unusual feat for Inuit boys. Besides, at issue
here is not whether the tales Minik told were fact or fantasy. At issue in this variation on Ovid's theme is the great distance between
the culture into which Minik was born and the one into which he
then crossed.

Sartre once said, "If I do not choose, that is still a choice."[3] This
may be true when a person is given a choice of alternatives and decides to select neither one, but Minik did not choose to become an
all-American boy. And although later it was his choice to return to
his first culture, he never chose to end up living a life "between two
extremes," as he described it (209).

It boggles the mind to think what it must have been like for Minik
to dock in Brooklyn on the last day of September 1897. His tribe
numbered 254 individuals. Now in a two-day period 30,000 people
visited Peary's ship. They came to inspect the meteorite Peary had
plucked from the northern landscape and to see the six Eskimos, as
Inuits were then called by others, whom he had brought with him.[4]
In Greenland Minik and his father lived in an igloo. Instead of snow
dwellings, here was the New York skyline. One can surmise that
Minik's first experience of New York resembled that of the baby
who, in William James's words, "feels it all as one great blooming,
buzzing confusion."[5] Many years later, however, he said, "Oh, I can
remember it very well, that day when we first saw the big houses
and saw so many people and heard the bells on the cars. It was like
a land that we thought must be heaven" (27).

But heaven it was not. "I beg to suggest to you," anthropologist
Franz Boas had written to Peary in 1896, "that if you are certain of
revisiting North Greenland next summer, it would be of the very
greatest value if you should be able to bring a middle-aged Eskimo

to stay here over winter. This would enable us to obtain leisurely certain information which will be of the greatest scientific importance" (25). Boas, who was on the staff of the American Museum of Natural History, wanted one Eskimo and got six. These six were taken from the boat directly to a set of rooms in the damp basement of the American Museum of Natural History. One month later they were all sent to Bellevue Hospital with pneumonia and by May of the next year, four of the six—one of them Minik's father—were dead. The fifth, a young man whose one ambition was to get home again, sailed on a ship bound for Greenland in July 1898. Thus did Boas end up with one Eskimo after all. And thus was the orphan Minik left to fend for himself in America.

Although there was no Dr. Itard or Professor Higgins to take him in charge, at first Minik thrived. Invited into the home of William Wallace, building superintendent of the museum, and treated as one of the family, Minik embarked on the life of a comfortably situated American boy, and in the process he became one. As he later reported, in 1899 the Wallaces enrolled him in a public school in the Bronx where "I learned to read and write and to know grammar and fractions and lots of other things" (46). But the Americanization of Minik did not just turn on his learning the English language or even on his forgetting his mother tongue—which he soon did. As a duck takes to water, he took to those All-American Boy activities of football, bicycle riding, ice skating, swimming, and catching snakes. In addition, he became close to his foster brother Willie and deeply attached to Mrs. Wallace, to whom he once said: "Minik's father is gone, but Aunt Rhetta is here" (44).

The Wallaces had a home in upstate New York where they spent summers and holidays and Minik and Willie roamed freely there. No wonder the press kept saying how lucky Minik was and how thankful he should be to have been removed from the barren Arctic! Harper commented that in both the city and the country "life was like a dream" for Minik (52). Although he was called upon from time to time to don native costume and sing his native songs, that dream was strictly American. True, when the Wallaces first took him in he cried constantly and was terrified of being sent back to the museum. Nevertheless, foster family, schooling, friends, sports, and the New York ethos itself all conspired to transform one small Inuit boy.

EXTERNAL AND INTERNAL CULTURE CROSSINGS

Minik's metamorphosis into a young American was as much a social enterprise as Malcolm's into a leader of his people or Eliza's
into a lady. Nonetheless, his transformation is different from theirs
in that Eliza and Malcolm traveled from one cultural group *inside* a
larger culture to another *within* that same culture, whereas Minik
moved into U.S. culture from the *outside*.[6]

Victor also entered his new culture from the outside, but the re-
semblance between his crossing and Minik's stops there. Despite
the fact that Victor was a biological human throughout the transformational process, his metamorphosis into a member of human
culture was like a cross-species rather than a cross-cultural change.
It was not, of course, the same as Gregor Samsa's fictional passage.
Gregor starts off human and turns into an insect, whereas biologi-
cally speaking Victor began human and remained so throughout
his life. Moreover, Gregor's metamorphosis is like Malcolm's from
model schoolboy to Harlem hustler, in that it represents what most
people would consider a fall from grace. Still, when Victor came
out of the woods he had not merely been living outside French culture; he had been living outside human culture itself—which is exactly where nonhuman species are thought to dwell.

Like Victor, newborns must journey *into* human culture. Once
that first great educational metamorphosis is accomplished, however, the transformations human beings undergo either involve
movement like Minik's *across* two distinct cultural wholes, or they
entail movement like Malcolm's between cultural groups *within* a
given cultural whole.[7] The term *cross-cultural* has long been used to
refer to the first sort of case but its range of application has gradually been expanded to cover both types of culture crossings. This
broader meaning of *cross-cultural* is being used here. To distinguish
between the two kinds of cross-cultural cases, the term *external* des-
ignates crossings that involve movement across distinct cultural
formations. The term *internal* in turn is reserved for the movement
between cultural groups existing within a larger cultural entity, as
exemplified by both Malcolm and Eliza Doolittle.[8]

Whether most external culture crossers sooner or later undergo
educational metamorphoses that transform them into members of
their new land's culture, as Minik's did, is an open question. Since

some immigrants want nothing so much as to hold onto their original cultures and others balk at the transformational process itself, it is safe to assume, however, that not all external culture crossers become brand new people. It is also safe to assume that not all those who make external crossings accomplish the task as easily as Minik did. Despite recurring ill health and the trauma of his father's death, his educational metamorphosis from an Inuit into an American boy seems to have proceeded apace.

No doubt, one reason why the course of Minik's crossing into U.S. culture ran so smoothly was that nobody in his foster family pressed the claims of Inuit culture upon him as Elaine Mar's mother pressed those of Chinese culture on her daughter, who in the last decades of the twentieth century was transformed from a small Chinese girl living in Hong Kong to an American schoolgirl. In her memoir *Paper Daughter*, Mar depicts a culture crossing fraught with pain and struggle. From her very first day in grade one of her U.S. public school she was taunted, tormented, and abused physically for her "chink eyes" and her inability to speak English.[9] Moreover, although she quickly learned that to be an American she must master the language of her classmates, dress like them, and be able to stand up for herself, her mother insisted on teaching her calligraphy, refused to send her to school in the kind of clothes the other children wore, and beat her when she did something of which the Chinese community in Denver might disapprove.

Studies of nineteenth-century immigration to America have shown how harsh and brutal the experience tended to be. The trip was long, the ships were crowded, food was in scarce supply, disease was rampant, and the New World presented a cruel face to strangers. For some end-of-twentieth-century immigrants the conditions of the literal crossing were unchanged, but for others— the Mar family among them—the literal crossing seems to have been a relatively routine affair. In Elaine's case, the harsh and brutal portion of her cultural crossing began after her arrival in the United States. Yet despite the blatant racism of her Denver schoolmates and the painful clashes between Chinese and U.S. culture, Elaine turned gradually into an American girl. In school she excelled. At home she spoke English, read the *Rocky Mountain News*, and watched *The Brady Bunch* on television. In the neighborhood she haunted stores featuring designer clothes and attended a Christian church with her one white, American-born friend.

Notice, however, that although Elaine Mar's culture crossing from Chinese to American girl falls squarely in the external category, the transformations she underwent afterward constitute internal crossings. In this respect her experience resembles that of other immigrants. A person does not stop undergoing educational metamorphoses once he or she is transformed into a member of a new culture—in other words, once an external culture crossing is made. But unless the individual returns home or moves to another country, whatever educational metamorphoses subsequently occur will constitute internal crossings within that culture.

The question remains of whether metamorphoses like Elaine's from an American schoolgirl into a Harvard graduate and like Malcolm's from a model American schoolboy into a Harlem hustler involve movement from one culture to another. Malcolm becomes a different person, but has this new person actually changed cultures? The answer depends on the way the term *culture* is defined. Reduce the term *culture* to *high culture* and this metamorphosis of his will not be considered a culture crossing, because the Harlem world he entered does not by this definition qualify as a culture. Nor, given this or any other narrow intellectualistic definition of *culture,* does the educational metamorphosis of Eliza Doolittle from a flower girl to a lady, or of Ildefonso, a twenty-seven-year-old deaf-mute illegal Mexican immigrant to the United States, count as a culture crossing.

When Ildefonso first encountered American Sign Language (ASL) interpreter and teacher Susan Schaller, he did not even know that such a thing as language existed.[10] All around him—in shops, on the street, at his uncle's house—people talked. In the classroom of the community college in California where he and Schaller met, Ildefonso was surrounded by signers but he had no idea what any of these people were doing. Of her first encounter with Ildefonso, Schaller said:

> I tried once more to explain without language that language existed, to explain without names that everything had a name. I failed, and his face showed that he knew he had let me down. We were only inches apart, but we might as well have been from different planets. (26)

Yet Ildefonso was no Martian. He was not even a Wild Child. True, he could not speak or comprehend language. Nevertheless, he had already undergone his first great metamorphosis. Ildefonso could walk, dress, feed himself, distinguish hot from cold, and even take a city bus. Just as the pre-Itard Victor somehow acquired the skills of survival in the wild, the pre-Schaller Ildefonso had managed to learn what he needed to know to survive inside human society. He may have inhabited its margins, but he nonetheless existed *within* its confines. Indeed, although it took Schaller a while to discover this, Ildefonso had his own small community.

By the time Schaller met Ildefonso's small circle of friends, he had broken the language barrier. His breakthrough, when it came, eerily resembled that of Jean Massieu, an eighteenth-century prelingual deaf boy known to Itard, and it was every bit as dramatic as Helen Keller's.[11] Suddenly, said Schaller, Ildefonso

> sat up, straight and rigid, his head back and his chin pointing forward. The whites of his eyes expanded as if in terror. He looked like a wild horse pulling back, testing every muscle before making a powerful lunge over a canyon's edge. My body and arms froze in the mime-and-sign dance that I had played over and over for an eternity. I stood motionless in front of the streaked *cat*, petted beyond recognition for the fiftieth time, and I witnessed Ildefonso's emancipation. . . .
>
> He slapped both hands flat on the table and looked up at me, demanding a response. "Table," I signed. He slapped his book. "Book," I replied. My face was wet with tears, but I obediently followed his pointing fingers and hands, signing "door," "clock," "chair." But as suddenly as he had asked for names he turned pale, collapsed, and wept. Folding his arms like a cradle on the table, he lay down his head. My fingers were white as I clutched the metal rim of the table, which squeaked under his grief more loudly than his sobbing. (44–45)

Shattering as it was, Ildefonso's insight was merely the first step of his eventual metamorphosis from a man without words to ASL speaker. It was not the metamorphosis itself, for he was not yet the new person he eventually became: a legal resident with a job at a private hospital tending gardens and creating new landscapes that are works of art.

After Ildefonso's educational metamorphosis was completed, he invited Schaller to an informal gathering of his peers. There an

astounded ASL teacher discovered that Ildefonso had all along
been a member of a group of men without language who were accustomed to communicating with one another in mime for hours
at a time:

> They told many border-crossing and border-patrol stories. The most
> breathtaking adventure involved a horse chase. . . . Each story con-
> tained a grain of information about how to enter white-man's land
> or avoid importation. No one could say to another, "Guess what I
> found out. In order to cross or stay legally. . . . " Instead a story that
> contained some fact had to be told and retold until someone else ei-
> ther understood the significance or at least understood that the teller
> knew something important. (182–83)

Define *culture* narrowly in relation to the arts, sciences, and
scholarship, and the community to which Ildefonso belonged at
the beginning of his metamorphosis has no culture. Adopt one or
another of the broad definitions of *culture* put forward by anthropologists and sociologists—for example, "the patterned behavior
of man in society"[12] or "a historically created design for
living"[13]—and both his transformation and Malcolm's transformation from model schoolboy to Harlem hustler constitute internal culture crossings.

Still, in the eyes of some a broad definition of culture has a fatal flaw: it allows animals as well as humans to have culture. Over
the centuries, one staple of Western culture has been the belief in
a sharp separation of humankind from the animals. Representing
nature as an arena of bodies without minds in which behavior is
instinctive and reason has no place—in other words, as the realm
of beasts who are presumed to lack intelligence—the West has
portrayed culture as a human creation in which reason holds
sway. If, however, the acquisition of traits and skills and the trans-
mission of them to the next generation is what culture is all
about—as broad definitions of culture affirm—it would seem that
animals possess it. After all, different chimpanzee groups dance
in different ways when it rains in the rainforests of Africa. And a
few years after a lone female macaque washed the dirt off a stash
of yams in water, all the female and young macaques in the troop
were doing the same.[14]

As it happens, the long-standing nature/culture dichotomy is untenable. When nature is defined in sharp contrast to culture, neither bird, beast, nor fish—neither wind, sun, nor rain—belongs to nature, for all have been affected by human culture. Nor is the idea of a human culture totally insulated from the influences of the so-called natural world of wind, sun, and rain borne out by the facts. Furthermore, to acknowledge the existence of animal culture is not in itself to say that animal cultures are as complex or sophisticated or original or creative as human cultures. Indeed, there is no reason why an adequate account of these radical changes should apply solely to human beings. True, the cases of educational metamorphoses introduced here are all instances of human transformations. But if it is shown that a parrot or chimpanzee or dolphin has undergone an educational metamorphosis, so be it.

ARE ALL WHOLE PERSON
TRANSFORMATIONS CULTURE CROSSINGS?

Does every educational metamorphosis constitute a culture crossing? The first great metamorphosis does not: although the end point of a newborn's transformation lies within human culture, the starting point lies outside it. Thus, a person's initial metamorphosis is neither an external nor an internal culture crossing. Furthermore, the educational transformation that many people experience in the process of dying does not seem to be a culture crossing either. Just as the starting point of the first great educational metamorphosis lies outside human culture, so presumably does the end state of this last great metamorphosis—namely, having died. Bracket the two transformations that serve as bookends to the educational changes that comprise a human life. Then, whether the other educational metamorphoses that a person undergoes constitute culture crossings will depend on one's definition of culture.

Take Eliza Doolittle's transformation from flower girl to lady. When the concept of culture is reduced to "high" culture, her radical identity change is not a culture crossing, for at Wimpole Street Eliza learns little, if anything, about art and literature, history and philosophy. When the term *culture* is defined broadly hers is, however, a thoroughgoing culture crossing. As a raw recruit's transformation into a United States Marine begins with a haircut and a new set of clothes, hers begins with a bath and a new wardrobe. "Take her away and clean her, Mrs. Pearce," says Higgins (21) when Eliza arrives on his doorstep asking for language lessons. "Take all her clothes off and burn them. Ring up Whiteley or somebody for new ones" (21). By the time her boot camp days are over, her walk and talk, her dress and table manners, her standards of cleanliness, her behavior toward old friends, her pastimes, and her self-image and self-respect have all changed.

Admittedly, the shift from one socioeconomic class to another is not usually called a culture crossing. The imagery invoked is more apt to be that of climbing a ladder than making a journey. Interestingly enough, however, our case studies consistently employ "travel talk." Of course they also use "self" and "identity" talk: the person becomes someone else, experiences inner conflict, has two compatible identities. But references abound to going on a journey, leaving family and friends behind, entering or not being able to enter a new world, and going back home again. Furthermore, the knowledge, skills, attitudes, values, ways of moving, modes of thinking, and patterns of behavior that Eliza acquires in the course of her metamorphoses do not merely constitute a design for living. Each one is itself an item of culture. These things comprise the cultural stock belonging to or laid claim to by the social class into which she crosses.

Whether Eliza's new inheritance is of greater value than the one she earlier received in Covent Garden; whether, as her father believes, it represents the appearance of wealth and not the genuine article; whether it includes liabilities such as snobbery and greed as well as assets are questions that need not be decided here. After all, the same kinds of questions can be asked about Minik's transformation into an All American Boy and his is a classic instance of culture crossing.

Rita's metamorphosis from working-class hairdresser to educated woman is more intimately bound up with "high" culture than Eliza's, but it also has to do with the acquisition of a wide range of cultural stock. Hence Rita's boast at the end of Willy Russell's play that she now knows not only how to talk and dress but what wine to buy, what plays to see, what papers and books to read (68). As if in confirmation of Russell's insight into the academy, an

American professor of sociology from a working-class background described drinking his first margarita. "Beer and whiskey and Seven-Up had been the drinks of choice in my working class environment. I started buying and listening to Joni Mitchell and jazz records. I had never heard of a bagel and cream cheese."[15] A working-class Smith College student talked about learning "to manage a knife and fork" and "how to approach soup."[16] And an Italian American from a working-class family said of her decision to attend the University of Illinois, "I understood that I would have to learn a new set of rules."[17]

In Emlyn Williams's play *The Corn Is Green*, a Welsh mining boy is turned into an Oxford man.[18] The details of his educational metamorphosis are obscured, however, when the play is read simply as an account of handing down "high" culture. After horrifying Miss Moffat, the school teacher who has devoted herself to educating him, by saying that he is going back to the coal mines, Morgan Evans tells her: "I do not want to learn Greek, nor to pronounce any long English words, nor to keep my hands clean" (55). To Miss Moffat's assistant he has already exclaimed:

> I'm surprised by meself, and shocked by meself! Goin' inside one o' them public houses and puttin' me nice clear boots on that dirty rail, and me dainty lad-fingers on that detestable mucky counter! Pourin' poison rum down me nice clear teeth—and spittin' in a spittoon— what's come over you, Morgan Evans? You come back to your little cage, and if you comb hair and wash hands and get your grammar right and forget you was once the Middle-weight Champion of the Glasynglo Miners, we might give you a nice bit of sewin' to do. (45–46)

Once again a fictional illustration of the cultural component of educational metamorphoses is matched by autobiographical accounts. Thus, even as a first grader Elaine Mar had a good idea of the kind of cultural stock she would have to acquire to become an American schoolgirl. She knew that she would have to learn to move in the "right" way, play the "right" games, talk about the "right" things, and have the "right" interests. Wanting desperately to be accepted—which she knew translated into being an American schoolgirl—she eventually went so far as to pretend that her parents were divorced.

Besides concealing the broad spectrum of cultural stock that a person acquires when undergoing a radical identity change, narrow definitions of culture obscure the social and cultural implications of the multiple educational metamorphoses we all experience. What happens to a culture when an individual who is undergoing an educational metamorphosis crosses into it? What happens to a culture when many individuals at approximately the same time experience personal transformations that allow them to cross into it?[19] Which cultural traits do those who undergo educational metamorphoses acquire? Are some traits more readily acquired than others? Are some kinds of crossings easier to make than others? How is a person who has undergone a change of identity received by his or her new culture? In what way is that individual treated by members of the old culture? With a narrow definition of culture, questions such as these cannot really be asked.

IMMIGRANTS ALL

When educational metamorphoses are seen as culture crossings and culture is defined broadly, just about everyone who undergoes an educational metamorphosis can be said to be an immigrant. To be sure, the first dictionary definition of *immigrant* is someone who has come to another country and settled there. However, the second definition sanctions a broader use of the term, according to which a plant or animal that has found a new habitat is an immigrant. In this second sense, those who make external culture crossings are immigrants and so are we all.

In a mid-twentieth-century study, historian Oscar Handlin provided an analysis of nineteenth-century immigration to the United States whose ring of truth for many of the culture crossers in our case studies confirms their immigrant status. Calling the story of that immigration "a history of alienation and its consequences," he said that it took people "out of traditional, accustomed environments and replanted them in strange ground, among strangers, where strange manners prevailed."[20] The immigrants lived in crisis, he wrote, because they were uprooted and because it was so difficult to adapt to the new conditions and challenges in the land they were entering.

Handlin pointed out that with customary modes of behavior inadequate and with old ties broken, the immigrants "faced the enormous compulsion of working out new relationships, new meanings to their lives, often under harsh and hostile circumstances" (5). Because "emigration had stripped away the veneer that in more stable situations concealed the underlying nature of the social structure" (5–6), the responses could not be easy or automatic. On the contrary, "every act was crucial, the product of conscious weighing of alternatives, never simple conformity to an habitual pattern" (6).

Handlin's analysis is echoed by a late-twentieth-century arrival to the United States from Mexico who said, "Immigration was like being born again—I had to learn to speak, I had to learn to eat and I had to learn to dress."[21] Moreover, the nineteenth-century immigrant experience is duplicated by many of the figures in our cases.

When Frank invites Rita to a dinner party at his house, she gets as far as his doorstep and then is unable to go inside. As she sees it, her dress is inappropriate, she has brought the wrong sort of wine, and she cannot speak their language. Academic men with working-class backgrounds worry in their turn about what drinks to order and what kind of vehicle to drive. For women academics, bankers, lawyers, and concert artists regardless of their class background, the smallest actions can be objects of conscious decision-making. Should I wear my hair long or short? Do I put on pants or a skirt to give this lecture or play this concerto? Do I smile or scowl at a department meeting? And a man born in Harlem who was teaching in a California University wrote:

> In fact, as a black college student you are expected to take on a new persona, one much more acceptable and less threatening to whites in society. There is an expectation that you will repudiate long held values and beliefs, even loved ones, in order to be accepted into a society which will not accept you any other way.[22]

There is often good reason to emphasize the differences between and among the varieties of educational metamorphoses and to treat these personal transformations/culture crossings as separate and distinct phenomena. Furthermore, culture crossers often seem to assume that their experiences are uniquely associated with their particular race, class, gender, ethnicity, or the like. However, the

similarities of experience that our cases reveal are too striking to be
ignored. Whether it is a class, race, gender, or ethnic crossing—or
some other kind entirely—belonging or fitting emerges as a central
concern for those who undergo educational metamorphoses, just
as it was for the nineteenth-century immigrants.

Thus, the coeditor of a volume of essays by academics from the
working class wrote, "As an undergraduate I only wanted to be accepted into the club, the university."[23] An author of one essay in
that anthology said of her college experience, "I had learned to buy
my classmates' thrown-away clothes at the local thrift store, and if
I kept my mouth shut I could pass as one of them in my classes."[24]
Another commented, "the working-class academic can never fully
'move in.'"[25]

In addition, an in-depth study of five women from "non-privi-
leged backgrounds" who enrolled in a special college program at
Smith College after many years outside the classroom reported that
their initial goal was cultural assimilation. Speaking of herself as
having "My Fair Lady expectations" and sounding very much like
Rita, one of them told her interviewer, "we had the faculty wine
and cheese party . . . and I was sitting there thinking of me not being able to get beyond, 'Hi, my name is Elinor.'"[26] And an African-
American academic explained: "I was convinced that . . . being
black and having any professional aspirations required one to re-
pudiate one's identity and to adopt the definitive social standard
against which all success would be measured."[27]

That Rita calls herself "a freak" and "a half-caste" (45) acquires
added significance when one learns that, in the early decades of the
twentieth century, Jewish immigrants to the United States wrote of
being "divided selves"[28]; that in the century's final days a Chinese
immigrant spoke of her family's household existing in "parallel
worlds"[29]; that in that same period a Japanese immigrant described
herself as "living in and between two cultures" and as leading a life
with "two halves that don't make a smooth whole."[30]

The fact that in the course of his educational metamorphosis
from a Mexican American boy into an American man Richard
Rodriguez turned his back on his home, his family, the Spanish
language, and the Mexican culture is in its turn illuminated by a
1938 analysis of second-generation immigrants to the United
States.[31] Rodriguez's memoir, *Hunger of Memory*, depicts an educa-

tional metamorphosis that enacts the American dream.³² When Richard entered first grade in a Sacramento, California, parochial school he was so timid, so shy, and so afraid to speak English that his teachers might easily have judged him to be as defective and uneducable as Ildefonso's parents judged their son and the scientists and philosophers judged Victor. As luck would have it, after observing this silent boy for six months or so, three teachers from Richard's parochial school arrived on his doorstep. "Do your children speak only Spanish at home, Mrs. Rodriguez?" asked the nuns. "Is it possible for you and your husband to encourage your children to practice their English when they are home?"

Rodriguez's parents immediately complied with the request. And so, he said, by the age of seven, "I came to believe what had been technically true since my birth: I was an American citizen" (22). He added, "The boy who first entered a classroom barely able to speak English, twenty years later concluded his studies in the stately quiet of the reading room in the British Museum" (43).

To explain an educational history replete with citations, medals, trophies, and the ever-present consciousness that "schooling was changing me" (45), Rodriguez invoked the concept of "the scholarship boy"—a working-class child who is a good student but has difficulty moving back and forth between the opposing worlds of school and home. Yet helpful as the idea surely is, the label allows Richard's ethnicity to fade out of the picture. If the Rodriguez family had remained in Mexico, an analysis of their son's educational metamorphosis might ignore his ethnicity with impunity. In that scenario, Richard would have had to undergo the same sort of class change that Rita does in order to become an educated person, but he would no more have had to become an assimilated Mexican than she has to become English, for he would already have been one. Because his parents immigrated to the United States the scholarship boy concept diminishes Rodriguez's accomplishment. The task he confronted was twofold: he had to change both his class identification and his ethnicity.

"How to inhabit two worlds at the same time was the problem of the second generation," wrote the author of the first comprehensive histories of European immigration to the United States. Historically, this problem was solved by escape. The son "wanted to forget everything: the foreign language that left an unmistakable trace in his English speech, the religion that continually recalled childhood struggles, the family customs that should have been the happiest of all memories."³³ "As I grew fluent in English," said Rodriguez, "I no longer could speak Spanish with confidence. I continued to understand spoken Spanish. And in high school, I learned how to read and write Spanish. But for many years I could not pronounce it" (28). Rodriguez's cultural location as a second generation immigrant provides a key to understanding not only his loss of the Spanish language but his feelings of pride when a teacher tells him that he was losing "all trace of a Spanish accent" (44). It places his mother's frequent complaints that the family was no longer close (51) in context. And perhaps above all, it helps explain how determined he was to escape.

GENDER CROSSINGS AS CULTURE CROSSINGS

The question remains of whether gendered educational metamorphoses constitute culture crossings. In search of an answer, consider the case of Isaac Bashevis Singer's Yentl.³⁴ Just as Ovid's "Pygmalion" is a myth of education par excellence, Singer's "Yentl the Yeshiva Boy" is a tale of a gender transformation extraordinaire.

Like "Pygmalion," "Yentl" can be read as a love story. As Ovid's sculptor fell madly in love with his statue, "a great love for Anshel [a.k.a. Yentl] took hold of Avigdor" the moment he found out that his Torah study partner was a woman. And we have Singer's word that Anshel was already in love's grip: "Without Avigdor the study house seemed empty. At night Anshel lay on her bench in the window, unable to sleep. Stripped of gabardine and trousers she was once more Yentl, a girl of marriageable age, in love with a young man who was betrothed to another" (169). Yet there is more to "Yentl the Yeshiva Boy" than the love angle. When her father is alive Yentl does what a woman is forbidden to do—she studies the Torah with him. "Yentl—you have the soul of a man," he tells her. "So why was I born a woman?" she asks. "Even Heaven makes mistakes," is his reply (160).

What exactly was Heaven's mistake?³⁵ Was the mistake simply to give Yentl the body of one gender and the soul of the other or might it have been something quite different? Could Heaven's mistake have been to create a world in which bodies and souls are labeled either male or female, but not both, and human traits and occupations are assigned to one or the other gender? Fables seldom give closure. It is enough that Singer's tale looks deeply into the way gender organizes human existence, for in so doing it reveals that gender crossings are indeed a species of culture crossing.

When Yentl's father dies, the marriage brokers flock to her door with offers, but Yentl turns them away:

> Inside her, a voice repeated over and over: "No!" What becomes of a girl when the wedding's over? Right away she starts bearing and rearing. And her mother-in-law lords it over her. Yentl knew she wasn't cut out for a woman's life. She couldn't sew, she couldn't knit. She let the food burn and the milk boil over; her Sabbath pudding never turned out right, and her *challah* dough didn't rise. (159)

So the young woman who used to dress up in her father's clothes and was even moved to smoke his pipe as he slept, sells her house, cuts off her braid, dons her father's garments, and goes out into the world in search of a yeshiva.

In short order Yentl finds a yeshiva and also the study partner with whom she falls in love. Now if this were an ordinary romance, Avigdor would soon realize that the young boy who likes to sew on his buttons and give him small gifts is really a young woman. After a brief lovers' quarrel, the two would marry. But just as Shaw knew that Eliza Doolittle would fare poorly in an alliance with Professor Higgins, Singer knew that marriage to Avigdor would ruin Yentl's life. "You could have married me," Avigdor says when he discovers the truth. "I wanted to study the Gemara and Commentaries with you, not darn your socks!" replies Yentl (187). "I wasn't created for plucking feathers and chattering with females" (185).

One would think that Avigdor or some other close observer of Yentl's gradual transformation into a Torah scholar would realize that Anshel is a woman. No beard. All those thoughtful little gifts. Choking on a sip of brandy. Sewing on Avigdor's buttons. Refusing to go to the baths or swim in the river. How could all these gender cues possibly be discounted? Reflecting on her own gender crossing, transsexual Kate Bornstein wrote that a person is assumed male until proven otherwise; that "It would take the presence of roughly four female cues to outweigh the presence of one male cue."[36] Confirming the old adage that clothes make the man, Yentl's cross-dressing trumps the intimations of femininity.

"What a strange power there is in clothing," thinks Avigdor after hearing Yentl's confession (188). And so there is. To achieve her desired transformation Eliza has to stop dressing like a flower girl and start looking and acting like a lady. Saying "I am educated now" (68), Rita assures Frank that at long last she knows what clothes to wear. En route to becoming a hustler, Malcolm Little buys himself a sky blue zoot suit with a hat to match. Desperately seeking acceptance as an American schoolgirl, Elaine Mar foregoes her lunches and spends the money on the clothes her mother will not buy her. In Victor's case the clothing issue is a bit more basic for, like a newborn, he must become accustomed to the very wearing of clothes. Yentl is used to wearing them, but as Victor's transformation into a creature of culture requires that he become a dresser, her transformation demands that she become a cross-dresser.

"How could you bring yourself to violate the commandment every day: 'A woman shall not wear that which pertaineth to a man'?" demands Avigdor (185). Yentl does not tell him what he already knows: that women are not allowed to attend a yeshiva and study the Torah. She does not take the trouble to remind him that were she to wear her own garb, she could not possibly become a respected Jewish scholar. She simply says, "I wasn't created for plucking feathers and chattering with females."

Shaking her head and folding her arms with an air of decision, the opera singing mother of George Eliot's *Daniel Deronda* tells her son:

> You are not a woman. You may try—but you can never imagine what it is to have a man's force of genius in you, and yet to suffer the slavery of being a girl. To have a pattern cut out—"this is the Jewish woman; this is what you must be; this is what you are wanted for; a woman's heart must be of such a size and no larger, else it must be pressed small, like Chinese feet: her happiness is to be made as cakes are, by a fixed receipt."[37]

Yentl's defense of her cross-dressing is not nearly so forceful. "I didn't want to waste my life on a baking shovel and a kneading trough," is what she says (184). To Avigdor's agonized plaint that they might have gotten married if she had told him all sooner, she responds that it would not have worked because "I am neither one nor the other" (184). Avigdor wonders if Yentl is a demon and she has a dream that she is both a man and a woman.

The psychic costs of Yentl's gender crossing are huge. Bornstein said of her own childhood, "I felt that there was something deeply wrong with me because I didn't feel like I was the gender I'd been assigned. I felt there was something wrong with me, something sick and twisted inside me, something very, very bad about me."[38] Like many of those today who become transgendered, Yentl thought "outlandish thoughts that brought her close to madness" (169). But she knows that she cannot go back to being a girl, that she can never again do without books as a woman must. Avigdor for the first time sees clearly "that this was what he had always wanted: a wife whose mind was not taken up with material things" (186). But who, if not Yentl, will do the housework? Shaw's crystal ball shows Freddie waiting hand and foot on Eliza, but it is hard to imagine Avigdor being willing to cook and clean. In fact, one can scarcely imagine either Avigdor or Yentl doing it. The painful truth is that neither one can envision a marriage between two Torah scholars. And so, saying "I don't know how to bake a pudding" (188), Yentl walks out of Avigdor's life.

Obviously, the changes undergone by the men and women who undergo gender reassignment therapy are very different from Yentl's. Yet they too are whole person or complete identity trans-formations, for the changes in these individuals are not just physiological. As Eliza Doolittle learns to walk, talk, dress, think, and act like a lady, transsexuals learn to walk, talk, dress, think, and act like members of what the dominant culture considers the "opposite" sex. True, those who undergo gender reassignment therapy may not make the hoped-for gender crossing successfully. But then, Eliza might in her turn have failed to become a lady. That for one reason or another some educational metamorphoses stop short of being full-fledged culture crossings does not negate the fact that most fall into this category.

In fact, the cultures into which an individual crosses supply the specific content of the radical identity changes composing that person's life. That is to say, the beliefs, skills, attitudes, values, worldviews, and the like that a person acquires in the course of an educational metamorphosis are all items belonging to the stock of the culture into which he or she enters. Just as Galatea becomes that cultural entity known as a woman when she turns into flesh and blood and not merely a generalized or generic human being, Eliza becomes that cultural entity known as an English lady and Malcolm becomes that cultural entity known as a model U.S. schoolboy. In the early twenty-first century it is commonplace to call things "cultural constructs." Because the phrase means different things to different people it can often be misleading. Nevertheless, the fact that every life is a series of radical changes of identity and that in these latter a particular culture's stock is acquired really does mean that every last one of us is a cultural construct. Immigrants all, we are indeed the products of all the cultures we have passed through as well as of those we have remained in.

NOTES

1. The material on Minik is based on Kenn Harper, *Give Me My Father's Body* (New York: Washington Square Press, 2000). Page references appear in parentheses in the text.

2. Jean-Jacques Rousseau, *Emile* (New York: Basic Books, 1979), 64.

3. Jean Paul Sartre, "Existentialism Is a Humanism," in *Existentialism from Dostoevsky to Sartre*, ed. Walter Kaufman (New York: Meridian Books, 1956), 305.

4. Harper wrote in his introduction, "While cognizant of the fact that today some Eskimos prefer to be known as Inuit, I have nonetheless used the term Eskimo throughout the book, and this is consistent with the usage in the historical sources listed and quoted" (xvi). Here, however, the term *Eskimo* is used only when the text appears to require it.

5. William James, *The Principles of Psychology*, vol. 1 (New York: Dover Publications, 1950) (1890), 488.

6. More precisely, he traveled into one cultural group within U.S. culture.

7. In *Routes* (Cambridge, MA: Harvard University Press, 1997), 2, anthropologist James Clifford expressed his concern with the concept of culture's "propensity to assert holism and aesthetic form, its tendency to privilege value, hierarchy, and historical continuity in notions of common 'life.'" It should therefore be noted that no assumptions of aesthetic form, value, hierarchy, historical continuity, or the like are being made here. As for holism, when the term "cultural whole" is used in these pages, it is assumed that what is considered to be a cultural whole will differ from one

context to another and that cultural wholes, like other wholes, can be divided into parts.

8. It should be noted that these cultural groups, like the cultures to which they belong, can have cultural groups within them.

9. M. Elaine Mar, *Paper Daughter* (New York: Perennial, 1999), 72.

10. Susan Schaller, *A Man without Words* (New York: Summit Books, 1991). Page references are in parentheses in the text.

11. For an account of Massieu see Oliver Sacks, *Seeing Voices* (Berkeley: University of California Press, 1989), 47.

12. David Bidney, *Theoretical Anthropology* (New York: Columbia University Press, 1953), 155.

13. Harry Hoijer, "The Relation of Language to Culture," in *Anthropology Today*, ed. A. L. Kroeber (Chicago: University of Chicago Press, 1953), 554.

14. Cynthia Mills, "Crashing the Culture Club," *Boston Globe*, November 26, 2002, C1, C3. According to Susan Blackmore, *The Meme Machine* (Oxford: Oxford University Press, 1999), 49, cases like these may look like "true cultural learning" but they are not. Her argument appears to rest, however, on the debatable point that although they are cases of social learning they are not cases of "true imitation."

15. Dwight Lang, "The Social Construction of a Working-Class Academic," in *This Fine Place So Far from Home*, ed. C. L. Barney Dews and Carolyn Leste Law (Philadelphia: Temple University Press, 1995), 171.

16. Patricia Clark Smith, "Grandma Went to Smith, All Right, but She Went from Nine to Five: A Memoir," in *Working-Class Women in the Academy*, ed. Michelle M. Tokarczyk and Elizabeth A. Fay (Amherst: University of Massachusetts Press, 1993), 135.

17. Nancy Lapaglia, "Working-Class Woman as Academics: Seeing in Two Directions, Awkwardly," in Dews and Law, *This Fine Place*, 179.

18. Emlyn Williams, *The Corn Is Green* (New York: Dramatists Play Service, Inc., 1938). Page references are in parentheses in the text.

19. It should be noted in passing that margaritas and bagels have not always been a part of the culture of the American academy.

20. Oscar Handlin, *The Uprooted* (Boston: Little, Brown, 1951), 4, 5. Page references appear in parentheses in the text.

21. Carola and Marcelo Suárez-Orozco, *Trans-formations* (Palo Alto, CA: Stanford University Press, 1995), 64.

22. Cecil E. Canton, "From Slaveship to Scholarship: A Narrative of the Political and Social Transformation of an African American Educator," in *The Politics of Survival in Academia*, ed. Lila Jacobs, José Cintrón, and Cecil E. Canton (Lanham, MD: Roman & Littlefield, 2002), 21.

23. Carolyn Leste Law, "Introduction," in Dews and Law, *This Fine Place*, 4.

24. Laurel Johnson Black, "Stupid Rich Bastards," in Dews and Law, *This Fine Place*, 22.

25. Mary Cappello, "Useful Knowledge," in Dews and Law, *This Fine Place*, 130.

26. Rosetta Marantz Cohen, "Class Consciousness and Its Consequences: The Impact of an Elite Education on Mature, Working-Class Women." *American Educational Research Journal*, vol. 356, no. 3 (1998), 361.

27. Cecil E. Canton, "From Slaveship to Scholarship," 21.

28. Robert E. Park, "Human Migration and the Marginal Man," in *Theories of Ethnicity*, ed. Werner Sollors (New York: Washington Square Press, 1996), 165.

29. Mar, *Paper Daughter*, 161.

30. Kyoko Mori, *Polite Lies* (New York: Fawcett Books, 1997), 257, 254.

31. Marcus Lee Hansen, "The Problem of the Third Generation Immigrant," in Sollors, *Theories of Ethnicity*, 202–15.

32. Richard Rodriguez, *Hunger of Memory* (Boston: David R. Godine, 1982). Page references are in parentheses in the text.

33. Hansen, "The Third Generation Immigrant," 204.

34. Isaac Bashevis Singer, "Yentl the Yeshiva Boy," in *Short Friday* (New York: Fawcett, 1986), 159–92. Page references are in parentheses in the text.

35. Note that she is not like transgendered Jennifer Finney Boylan who from age three was aware of being in the wrong body. Jennifer Finney Boylan, *She's Not There* (New York: Broadway Books, 2003).

36. Kate Bornstein, *Gender Outlaw* (New York: Vintage Books, 1995), 26.

37. George Eliot, *Daniel Deronda* (London: Penguin, 1986), 694.

38. Bornstein, *Gender Outlaw*, 12.

Varieties of
Identity Transformations

A MOTHERING METAMORPHOSIS

Did Galatea become a different person after the birth of Paphos? Will Rita turn into someone else if she decides to have a baby? Eliza makes a class crossing, Yentl makes a gender crossing, Minik makes an ethnic crossing, but this list does not begin to capture all the varieties of educational metamorphoses. There are "hybrid" types like Rita's and Richard Rodriquez's: her transformation into an educated person is both a class and a gender crossing and his is both a class and an ethnic crossing. There are also educational metamorphoses occasioned by events in the life cycle.

"I used to be a reasonably careless and adventurous person, before I had children; now I am morbidly obsessed by seat belts and constantly afraid that low flying aircraft will drop on my children's school," writes Margaret Drabble.[1] Poet Adrienne Rich reports that after the birth of her first child she was so racked with maternal guilt that she asked, "daily, nightly, hourly, Am I doing what is right? Am I doing enough? Am I doing too much?"[2] And Rosamund, the protagonist of Drabble's 1965 novel *The Millstone*—or *Thank You All Very Much* as it was called in the United States—says:

Love had isolated me more securely than fear, habit or indifference. There was one thing in the world that I knew about, and that one thing was Octavia. I had lost the taste for half-knowledge. George, I could see, knew nothing with such certainty. I neither envied nor pitied his indifference, for he was myself, the self that but for accident, but for fate, but for chance, but for womanhood, I would still have been.[3]

Existentialist philosopher Simone de Beauvoir took a dim view of motherhood. In *The Second Sex* she wrote: "Maternity is usually a strange mixture of narcissism, altruism, idle day dreaming, sincerity, bad faith, devotion, and cynicism."[4] Second wave feminists echoed her sentiment, with one saying, "The heart of woman's oppression is her childbearing and childrearing roles,"[5] and another insisting that motherhood represents "the annihilation of women."[6] Be this as it may, after the birth of her baby and through the course of her infant's life-threatening illness and the obstacles presented by the British medical establishment, Rosamund becomes a new person.

Says Drabble's diffident heroine:

> Hitherto in my life I had most successfully avoided the bond that links man to man, though I had paid it some lip service; the closest and most serious connections I had ever known had been with people like Joe, Roger, and indeed George, connections which seem trivial enough to recount but upon which I had expended a good deal of attention as idle, refined, educated single girls will: and, fool that I was, I thought that this was what life was about. (59)

It scarcely needs saying that Rosamund's mothering transformation does not represent a formative event in every human life in the way the first great educational metamorphosis does. Indeed, Rosamund does not represent all mothers: not even all new mothers who, like her, are white, middle class, unmarried, and English. On the other hand, at the end of the twentieth century a sociologist asked undergraduate students in the United States if they believed there is a "great divide" between parents and nonparents. Those who were not parents said, "Of course not," and those who were parents said, "Absolutely."[7] In the conclusion to her study of motherhood she wrote, "The fact is, the presence of children does not simply 'add' to the lives of adult caregivers; it transforms those lives utterly—for better, for worse, and in all manner of subtle and tricky ways too complex to inventory."[8]

As for Rosamund, many women will find familiar her disconcerting realization: "I could feel that my own personal morality was threatened: I was going to have to do things that I couldn't do. Not things that were wrong, nothing as dramatic as that, but things that were against the grain of my nature" (p. 62). Many will experience the extraordinary pleasure she felt when she first looked into her baby's eyes: "I sat there looking at her, and her great wide blue eyes looked at me with seeming recognition, and what I felt is pointless to try to describe. Love, I suppose one might call it, and the first of my life" (p. 86). Many will feel dread as never before "on another's behalf" (p. 101) and will nod in agreement that "responsibility lay so heavy on me that I could not take what I knew to be the truth" (p. 131). And some will finally learn what it is to worry.

The author of a classic study of motherhood reported one woman saying, "It's really like living in a different world,"[9] And, indeed, Drabble's novel depicts an educational metamorphosis that is as much a culture crossing as Eliza's, Minik's, or Rita's. At its onset Rosamund reports, "I saw that from now on I . . . was going to have to ask for help, and from strangers too: I who could not even ask for love or friendship" (61). When at the very end Rosamund sees George for the first time since Octavia was conceived, he tells her that her hair is turning gray. "It must be worry," she says. "Worry has driven me to it." "What do you worry about?" asks George, who has absolutely no idea that the woman to whom he is speaking has crossed over into a different culture and left him behind. "Everything," she says from the other side of a divide whose pains and pleasures are denied him. "Everything" (140).

Lest it be thought that to single out mothering as a type or category of educational metamorphosis makes women the prisoners of biology, let it be noted that the identity change under discussion has a cultural basis, not a biological one. It is a function of cultural practices rather than of biological reproduction. Thus although a woman who bears a child but gives it up for adoption at birth may undergo a whole person change, it is not likely to be the same kind as Rosamond's. On the other hand, an adoptive mother who enters wholeheartedly into her society's cultural practices of mothering may well experience this variety of transformation. So, too, can those who serve as surrogate mothers in the old-fashioned sense of acting in the manner of a mother without actually being that child's biological or adoptive parent.

Furthermore, there is no reason to suppose that the boundless love, the worry, the guilt, the heavy sense of responsibility, the protectiveness, the need to reach out to others that characterize Rosamund's metamorphosis are gender-specific. True, Rosamund seems to think that her "womanhood" is essential to the radical change of self she experiences. Moreover, George is never given the chance to be transformed by his daughter Octavia's birth. For better or worse—and Drabble makes it difficult for readers to decide which—Rosamund does not tell him that the small child he sees for the first time at book's end is his. Nonetheless, men as well as women can and do develop these dispositions, which is to say that both sexes can undergo one or another variety of mothering metamorphosis.[10]

A COMING OF AGE METAMORPHOSIS

Becoming a mother is not the only event in the human life cycle that is apt to give rise to an educational metamorphosis. In addition to the metamorphoses occasioned by being born and by the process of dying, there are, for example, the transformations of a small girl into a young woman and of a small boy into a young man.

Coming of age stories abound, and although many of them record hardships, their authors are apt to confess to having nevertheless been happy or lucky or both.[11] Consider, however, the educational metamorphosis of Mark Mathabane from a small black South African boy living under apartheid—a Kaffir boy, to use the derogatory term that most white South Africans employed when Mark was growing up—into an educated young man in the English-speaking tradition.

No one could say that Mark was lucky to have been born in South Africa's most desperate ghetto in 1960 or that his coming of age metamorphosis was on balance a happy affair. At age six, wrote Mark in *Kaffir Boy*, "I was called upon to deal with constant terror."[12] For him, apartheid meant "hate, bitterness, hunger, pain, terror, violence, fear, dashed hopes and dreams" (x). It meant living in a shack, wearing rags, and going without breakfast and lunch. It meant police raid after police raid, week in and week out. And it meant endless struggles with an often drunk and violent father who was "force-feeding us tribalism" (32).

Still, luck is relative. A person can be lucky in relation to some things, for instance love, and not others. Moreover, one may be lucky in comparison to some people and unlucky in comparison to others. It cannot be denied that Mark was very, very unlucky compared to most boys growing up in the United States or the United Kingdom. Yet in comparison to the children in his ghetto he had a little bit of luck in the form of a mother who not only loved him dearly but valued schooling, a grandmother who took it upon herself to show him another world, and prodigious intellectual and athletic talents of his own.

School was an important educational agent in Mark's metamorphosis, although not exactly a benign one. If the government had had its way, Mark might never have been admitted to school: a birth certificate was required and by the time a white nun took up his cause he had already been denied one for a year or more. If Mark had had his way, he would never have attended school: he belonged to a gang of roving boys whose curriculum consisted in fighting, stealing, and rebelling and on the day he was to register, he tried so hard to escape that his mother and grandmother had to tie up his hands and feet and drag him there. And if his father had had his way, Mark would never have registered for school: "Why doesn't he want me to go to school?" Mark asked his mother after his drunken father beat her up for having enrolled their son. She replied, "He says he doesn't have money to waste paying for you to get what he calls a useless white man's education" (131–32).

According to one commentator, multiculturalists are apt to say, "love me, love my culture."[13] Mark's father shared the sentiment. At a surprisingly early age, however, Mark came to believe that to escape apartheid he would have to reject his ancestors' tribal

traditions. "Apartheid," he says "had long adulterated my her-
itage and traditions, twisted them into tools of oppression and indoctrination" (xi).

In outright defiance of his father, Mark promised his mother to
attend school. This vow was another bit of luck, for his first full day
there was a veritable nightmare and he might have left on the spot
had he not given his word. Incredibly, the whippings by teachers
continued throughout the school year even though Mark was first
in his class with test scores far above those of the runners-up.
Moreover, as the years passed and Mark stayed at the top of his
class, the whippings became more severe—all because he did not
have the money to pay for school fees, books, and uniforms. Time
and again, however, Mark's mother persuaded him to suffer the
pain being inflicted on him and remain in school. Finally the day
came when his grandmother obtained permission for him to accompany her to work.

As school was one educational agent responsible for Mark's
coming of age metamorphosis, the liberal white South African
community was another. Mark first felt its educational effects the
day his grandmother took him to Johannesburg where she worked
in the garden of a Mrs. Smith. Mark's entrance into the city is reminiscent of Minik's arrival in New York City: "As the bus droned
past Alexandria's boundaries, I glued my eyes to the window, anticipating my first look at the white world. What I saw made me
think I had just made a quantum leap into another galaxy" (185).
What made it so memorable, however, is that from the bus window, Mark saw white schoolchildren for the first time.

Tennis may be what ultimately saved Mark—he himself called
his achievements in that sport his "passport to freedom" (xi)—yet
it is scarcely an exaggeration to say that a white schoolboy sealed
his fate. For on this trip to the white man's world, Mrs. Smith's son
Clyde said to him:

> My teachers tell us that Kaffirs can't read, speak or write English like
> white people because they have smaller brains, which are already
> full of tribal things. My teachers say you're not people like us, be-
> cause you belong to a jungle civilization. That's why you can't live
> or go to school with us, but can only be our servants. (192)

Mr. Ostrowski told Malcolm Little that he could not be a lawyer and the boy left school for good. In Mark's case a casual racist comment pointed him in an opposite direction. He wrote:

> The remark that black people had smaller brains and were thus incapable of reading, speaking or writing English like white people had so wounded my ego that I vowed that, whatever the cost, I would master English, that I would not rest till I could read, write and speak it just like any white man, if not better. Finally, I had something to aspire to. (192)

The "something" Mark aspired to was not what his schooling aimed at. His father may have called it a white man's education, but schooling for black South Africans was not modeled on the education given to whites. The country's school system did not have two separate but equal tracks. No, Mark's schooling was designed by white men for black children and its object was to prepare them "to acquire a solid foundation in tribal life" (193). Consequently, the teaching of English was minimal—"all talk, all teaching, all thinking for that matter, was in Tsonga" (194). Books like *Treasure Island*, the volume that Mrs. Smith gave Mark by way of apology for Clyde's behavior, were not in the school library.

Mark singled out his first day in the white world as a "turning point" (x), for from that day he set his sights high: "To learn to express my thoughts and feelings effectively in English became my main goal in life. I saw command of the English language as the crucial key with which to unlock doors leading into that wonderful world of books" (193). Once he became single-minded, he quit his gang of boys for good. And shortly before he entered secondary school, for which he won a government scholarship, Mrs. Smith gave him an old wood tennis racket. "Practice hard," she told him. "One day I want to read about you in the papers, as our next Arthur Ashe" (208).

Mark did practice hard, and his tennis prowess together with his great intellectual achievements ultimately earned him his "freedom."[14] Torn to the end by love of family and the belief that in going to the United States he had a "duty to my race and country to use my life in a meaningful way, to see my successes and failures as the successes and failure of the black race" (348), in

September 1978 Mark left South Africa to study and play tennis in an American college.

EDUCATED WOMEN METAMORPHOSES

Knowledge of the life cycle does not allow us to identify all the educational metamorphoses that shape human lives—not even all the important ones. For instance, it does not tell us that in becoming an artist a person may be totally transformed. It does not record the educational metamorphoses that can be occasioned by divorce, rape, a death in the family, or even by the higher education of women.

Universities as well as yeshivas were originally established by men for men. Although the entrance of women students into higher education in the nineteenth century is sometimes portrayed as a natural occurrence whose time had come, when American colleges began admitting women into what had been a man's world, members of both sexes protested that a higher education would "unsex" women. Indeed, the women's colleges established in that period were specifically designed to protect "femininity."[15] And the fear of lost femininity was not limited to the nineteenth-century United States. Commenting on the women who attended Oxford University lectures with him in the 1920s, the author of *The Corn Is Green* wrote: "Lectures were dull and not helped by the many tricolored and bespectacled undergraduettes who seemed to write down everything that was said, including 'good morning,' and did nothing to belie the legend that they were of the third gender."[16]

In the late twentieth-century England of Russell's play, Rita suffers no anxiety that she will become unsexed—or, in twenty-first-century terminology, ungendered. But her husband is another matter. Believing that his wife's interest in getting an education is unwomanly and unable to find the words to tell her, Denny burns her books when she goes back on the contraceptive pill.

Rita herself appears quite unconscious of making a gender crossing. Ask her and she will say that being a woman has been no barrier whatsoever to her continuing education. Whether or not she is correct, the gift Frank gives her in the play's last scene signifies that in becoming educated she has attained the unenviable status of a living contradiction.

> Rita: An educated woman, Frank, an' this is what you call a scholarly neckline?

> Frank: When choosing it I put rather more emphasis on the word woman than the word educated. (73)

Yentl lives in a society held hostage to the old male-female gender stereotypes. In her world, for a woman to become educated she must literally masquerade as a man. In Rita's more broad-minded environment, higher education has been extended to women. But although Rita does not have to be a cross dresser to get a higher education, once educated she will have to find clothes to wear and ways to behave that block the cultural perception that thinking logically and analytically is something women never do.

An important late-twentieth-century discovery about gender was that traits that can in fact be possessed by both men and women are apt to be appraised differently in the two sexes. Take aggressiveness. In most of the nooks and crannies of Western culture, this item of cultural stock is considered an asset when possessed by males: an aggressive man is thought to be masculine, heroic, capable, strong, forceful, manly. In females, however, it tends to be seen as a liability: an aggressive woman is said to be pushy, bitchy, domineering, obnoxious, emasculating. Take caring and compassion. These are "genderized" in the opposite direction: females are expected to possess these items of cultural stock and are admired for exhibiting them. On the other hand, caring, compassionate men are apt to be viewed with suspicion. Indeed, he who possesses these items of cultural stock will likely be called soft or effeminate.

To succeed at her studies, Rita must button up her sentiments, reign in her emotions, curb her feelings, and replace all of the above with the same kind of logic, reason, objectivity, distance, and disinterestedness that the scholars and scientists who determined Victor's fate displayed. Her problem is not that she cannot acquire the cultural stock in question. It is that in the educated culture into which she crosses—a culture that is white and upper-middle-class as well as male—this stock is assumed to belong to men. In other words, Rita's problem is that the gender stereotypes of both the culture she inhabits and the one into which she is headed place her in a double bind.

Frank knows this. When he separates the two words *educated* and *woman* he acknowledges that to be a woman an individual has to be feminine and that for her to be an educated person in his culture she must not be feminine.[17] He realizes that in becoming educated Rita must acquire cultural stock—ways of thinking and seeing the world—that her culture values for men only. But then, to appear womanly in the culture's eyes, she must not think in the way an educated person is supposed to. And on the other hand, if she appears educated, she will no longer be judged a "true" woman.

Educating Rita resembles Rodriguez's memoir in making social class the salient issue. To be sure, Russell is quoted in an introduction to his script as saying, "I tried very hard to write a love story" (xv). But Rita does not fall in love with her tutor. She falls in love with literature as defined by the academy and with the culture of the educated class. Just as Elaine Mar knows that to become an all-American girl she must shed her Chinese identity, Rita knows that to become the kind of person who is welcome in the academy she must cast off her working-class identity. Frank's gift of an ultrafeminine dress signifies Russell's awareness that Rita's gender as well as her social class is at odds with the demands of higher education.

Actually, Rita's decision to study English literature instead of, say, mathematics or engineering or law, may save her from the slings and indignities that plague many women students in the academy. Higher education's fields of study differ in their degree of genderization and English is considered to be fairly low on the scale of masculinity.

In the case of the law, two studies of the experiences of women students starkly confirm the double bind's existence. In law school, wrote Mona Harrington, "The professors, particularly in first-year courses, are missionaries. Their mission is to reach into the skull of every student and reshape the mind inside."[18] What educational transformation does law school have in store? The average law professor would say that just as a medical school turns its students into doctors, law school's job is to teach each student to think like a lawyer. But there is more to the story. Harrington, herself a 1960

Harvard Law School graduate, wrote that although in 1990, 42 percent of the entering class were women, "in the inner life of the school, at its intellectual center, a male identity persisted" (47). And law professor Lani Guinier described her student experience in the mid-1970s as "the transformation from Black woman to gentleman law student."[19] Indeed, the title of a book she coauthored about law students is *Becoming Gentlemen.*[20]

Guinier recalled a Business Units 1 professor "who addressed all of us, male and female, as *gentlemen.*"[21] When she returned to that law school ten years later to participate in a symposium, the walls of that Business Units I classroom were still adorned "by the traditional larger-than-life portraits of white men."[22]

Almost all the women law school graduates in Harrington's study also mentioned the portraits:

> High on the walls of the classrooms, large oil paintings of legal luminaries stare down—bewigged English jurists, black-robed American judges, deans, professors, and other notable lawyers in three-piece suits, vests stretching across ample stomachs. Until 1988, when several students succeeded in a campaign to mount some portraits of women, this iconography of the law, which extends out of the classrooms, down long corridors, and around the high-ceilinged library, was wholly male. (45)

The male portraits and the masculine form of address are the least of a female student's worries, however. The problem for women is that their presence "is somehow out of keeping with the workings of the law." It is that "long tradition connects legal analysis with intellectual traits generally ascribed to men" (47).

Research done suggests that whether a woman is African American, Asian American, Native American, or Caucasian American, her legal education in the United States will involve a gender crossing. The gentleman she is expected to become is not a Colonel Pickering who tips his hat and opens doors for ladies. He is someone more like Professor Higgins: a person who is at once tough and sharp, objective and combative, aggressive and emotionally detached.

If things go according to schedule, a woman law student will undergo a radical identity change, for the cultural stock that the legal profession bequeaths to her includes forms of speech and modes of conducting business that are foreign to her. Like Rita, a female law student may have no idea that her gender actually influenced the course of her education to that point. And even supposing that in a particular woman's case it did not, the gendered nature of the law school experience is still not easily dismissed.

Taking seriously its mission to turn out gentlemen, law school is as intent on eliminating from its student body cultural stock historically and culturally associated with women as it is on preserving and fostering that associated with men. Compassion is eradicated, a third-year white woman told an interviewer for the Guinier et al. study (52). Emotion in an argument is a minus, said a third-year Latino man (53). "The law school culture—meaning what gets measured, how people are rewarded, and what kinds of mistakes are not forgiven—represents a set of beliefs and values that emphasizes aggressiveness," wrote the authors of *Becoming Gentlemen* (9). "Women are under perpetual suspicion of intellectual and temperamental softness," wrote Harrington (47).

Ask any law student and you will be told that law school is no picnic. There is too much work. Frequently the preferred method of teaching is intimidation. The competition is fierce. A female law student will have the added burden of finding herself caught, like Rita, in a double bind. To become a lawyer she must think like a man, talk like a man, conduct business like a man—or, to be more precise, like the cultural stereotype of a white, upper middle class man. Yet for making these portions of cultural stock her own she may be despised, disparaged, and degraded.

Being logical, being analytic, being combative, being competitive, showing that you can reason with the best of them: every last one of the qualities that law school expects both male and female law students to acquire is genderized in favor of males—which means that females who acquire them risk denigration. The behavior of the male law students bears this out. Many of the women interviewed for the Penn study described their first year as "a radical, painful, or repressive experience" (48). Even some of those who did well academically "did not recognize their former selves which they perceived as submerged in the pursuit of succeeding as a 'social male.'" Thus, one woman law student felt silenced by a group of law fraternity men "who call you man-hating lesbian, or feminist— as though those are bad—if you are too outspoken" (48). When the men call a woman a "feminazi dyke" or a "man-hating lesbian" for displaying the very kind of thinking and speaking that is expected of lawyers, they are not just vilifying her: they are casting doubt on her femininity—in fact, on the femininity of all women who speak out in class.

According to a third-year male student, "Whenever men at the law school open their mouths, something horrendous about women seems to come out. There are so many such incidents that to try and list them would be futile. Disparaging remarks about women's bodies, menstrual cycles, sexual orientation, etc., are the rule" (62).

In structure if not substance, the plight of women law students resembles that of Oedipus. He wanted to marry Jocasta, not his mother. But as the fates would have it, Jocasta was his mother, and so in doing the one act, he did the other. A woman in law school wants to think like a lawyer, in fact be a lawyer. She probably does not want a gender change, but this appears to come with the territory—as do a race and class change for many women. But this means that in becoming a lawyer she will perforce become a "gentleman." Does this amount to a culture crossing? Any number of scholars have called the very idea of a woman's culture essentialist and have denied that women and men have different cultures. Yet to the extent that women in law school acquire new ways of walking, talking, dressing, thinking, and acting, they are indeed making culture crossings.[23]

A MILITARY METAMORPHOSIS

Knowledge of the life cycle does not inform us either about the radical change a young man undergoes when he enters a military culture. "I lost my baby boy when you went to war. You were once so sweet and gentle and now you are an angry and unhappy man," Anthony Swofford's mother told her son.[24] An unhappy, angry, brutalized young man is probably not what Swofford expected to turn into when he joined the Marine Corps. Yet anger, brutality, and unhappiness were prime ingredients of the new self created by the educational metamorphosis he underwent in the military.

In *Jarhead*, Swofford's 2003 memoir, this lance corporal in a United States Marine Corps scout/sniper platoon during the Gulf

War wrote that as early as age fourteen he began to dream of being a marine: "I was a boy falling in love with manhood. I understood that manhood had to do with war, and war with manhood, and to no longer be just a son, I needed someday to fight. I thought of the marines constantly" (128). Fourteen may sound a bit young to be seduced by a branch of the military, yet in 2004 the city of Chicago alone had 10,000 teenage "cadets" in its elementary, middle, and high schools. The official rationale for the after-school military programs seems to have been that they would provide citizen and leadership training, but according to one local school council member, his school's program "ended up just being about obedience."[25]

Interestingly enough, in his highly praised and widely read 1910 essay, "The Moral Equivalent of War," William James called obedience to command a "martial virtue."[26] Besides presenting as vivid an account of a military educational metamorphosis as one might hope to read, *Jarhead* provides insight into the way it and the three other presumed virtues of war that James wanted to preserve— obedience to command, intrepidity, contempt of softness, and surrender of private interest—translate into practice.

Consider first obedience to authority. Swofford reported that on his second day in boot camp,

> Burke punched the recruit square on his forehead. He swayed but his knees did not give. The recruit had made the mistake of using personal pronouns, which the recruit is not allowed to use when referring to the drill instructor or himself. The recruit is the recruit. The drill instructor is the drill instructor or sir.
>
> Burke surveyed the platoon, hands clasped behind his back.
>
> He yelled, addressing us all, "I am your mommy and your daddy! I am your nightmare and your wet dream! I am your morning and your night! I will tell you when to piss and when to shit and how much food to eat and when! I will teach you how to kill and how to stay alive! I will forge you into part of the iron fist with which our great United States fights oppression and injustice! Do you understand me, recruits?" (28)

Consider next contempt of softness. After boot camp and six weeks of barracks-duty training, Swofford was sent to the infantry. This, he realized, was "the real Marine Corps" (47). Upon entering room 325, he saw a large crowd gathered around an unmade rack, my rack. One marine was biting his fist as another used a propane torch to heat wire hangers bent to form the letters USMC. I dropped my gear and watched.

Someone said, "Fucko is here."

When the hangers pulsed red-hot, the branding marine shoved the four-letter contraption against the other marine's outer calf. The marine bit his fist until he broke skin and began to bleed. Tears streamed from his eyes and the room filled with the dank stink of his flesh. I vomited into the shitcan and the room erupted in cheers. Before I could speak, the men piled on top of me and bound my hands behind my back with an electrical extension cord and gagged me with dirty skivvies. (50–51)

Now consider sacrifice of self. Swofford commented on what he saw when his battalion finally crossed into Kuwait:

I've never seen such destruction. The scene is too real not to be real. Every fifty to one hundred feet a burnt-out and bombed-out enemy vehicle lies disabled on the unimproved surface road, bodies dead in the vehicles or blown from them. Dozens, hundreds, of vehicles with bodies inside or out. . . . This is war, I think. I'm walking through what my father and his father walked through—the epic results of American bombing, American might. The filth is on my boots. I am one of a few thousand people who will walk this valley today. I am history making. Whether I live or die, the United States will win this war. (221–22)

James believed that a sharp line can be drawn between the "higher" military sentiments and the "bestiality" of war. Whether or not it can be in theory, at least three of James's four martial virtues were laced with bestiality in Swofford's actual experience.

Swofford's educational metamorphosis into a Marine Corps sniper is, of course, no more universal than is Rosamund's mothering metamorphosis. Even as mothers are not all transformed in her image, military recruits—be they rich or poor, elementary school cadets or college graduates—do not all become brutalized and brutalizing cogs in a machine.[27] Yet his experience resonates with other firsthand accounts of war. "I began to detect with a kind of horror that I was becoming inured to cruelty and not

above practicing it myself on occasion," wrote philosopher
J. Glenn Gray about his World War II experiences.[28] Long after he
was a bombardier in that same war, peace activist and historian
Howard Zinn wrote in a memoir of his own: "The more I read, the
more I thought about World War II, the more I became convinced
that the atmosphere of war brutalizes everyone involved."[29] The
difference between these acutely self-aware accounts and Swofford's equally perceptive one is that in his case the brutalization
began long before he reached a battlefield.

As the world changes, so of course will the varieties of military
educational metamorphoses. One wonders if as more and more
women become military recruits, they will undergo the same
kinds of transformation that men now do or if there will be clear
gender differences. One wonders if as war itself is transformed,
military metamorphoses will become less brutalizing. And one
wonders if and how a person whose life has been shaped by a
brutalizing culture crossing such as Swofford's can make a culture crossing like Rosamund's.

POLITICAL METAMORPHOSES

The military can be responsible for educational metamorphoses
and so can those broad-based political movements that seek to
change the world. Take, for example, the Women's Movement, the
Civil Rights Movement, and the Native American Movement in the
United States in the 1960s and 1970s. The extent to which they succeeded in transforming reality will be debated for years to come,
but it is beyond dispute that many individuals who came under
their sway were radically transformed.

In a 1976 essay philosopher Sandra Bartky drew upon her personal experience to articulate what it then meant to become a feminist.[30] Although her title, "Toward a Phenomenology of Feminist
Consciousness," suggests that the change feminism brought about
in her and many of her cohorts was something less than the whole
person transformation required by an educational metamorphosis,
her account of what happens when a person becomes a feminist fits
the bill.

"To be a feminist," Bartky wrote, "one has first to become one. For many feminists, this involves the experience of a profound personal transformation." She elaborated that the feminist

> changes her behavior. She makes new friends; she responds differently to people and events; her habits of consumption change; sometimes she alters her living arrangements or, more dramatically, her whole style of life. She may decide to pursue a career, to develop potentialities within herself which had long lain dormant or she may commit herself to political struggle. (11)

The experience Bartky described so well was a full-blown educational metamorphosis. She made no claim that all feminists of her era had undergone whole person transformation like hers, but it is clear from her account that those for whom her "morphology of feminist consciousness" rang true did not merely come to believe in equal pay for men and women or in some abstract concept of women's rights. They embraced new ways of being in the world. Their design for living was fairly general; it did not require a woman to burn a bra, forswear lipstick, become a lesbian, or perform any other specific actions. Causing her to "see things differently" (21), it did, however, transform day-to-day living "into a series of invitations to struggle" (20). Enabling her to "make out possibilities for liberating collective action and for unprecedented personal growth," it counterbalanced her feelings of alienation from established society "by a new identification with women of all conditions and a growing sense of solidarity with other feminists" (21).

Is it accurate to call Bartky's metamorphosis "political"?[31] It is certainly not narrowly so in the sense of having to do with party politics or governmental affairs. But in the broad sense of the term implicit in the once popular feminist slogan, "The personal is the political," the label seems apt. For the change of identity that Bartky described involves understanding power relationships at home and in the world, perceiving that what seem to be idiosyncratic shortcomings might be systematically related to gender roles and stereotypes, deciding when to struggle and when prudence should prevail, and knowing that social reality needs to be transformed.

Consider now the personal transformation that the renowned African-American writer Alice Walker underwent in the 1960s and poignantly described in *In Search of Our Mothers' Gardens*:

> It was just six years ago that I began to live. . . . Until that time my mind was locked apart from the outer contours and complexion of my body as if it and the body were strangers. The mind possessed both thought and spirit—I wanted to be an author or a scientist—which the color of the body denied. I had never seen myself and existed as a statistic exists, or as a phantom. In the white world I walked, less real to them than shadow; and being young and well hidden among the slums, among people who also did not exist—either in books or in films or in the government of their own lives—I waited to be called to life. And, by a miracle, I was called.[32]

Six years earlier Walker's mother had bought a television set in order to watch soap operas. On the day that Dr. Martin Luther King Jr.'s face appeared on its screen—on the day "the Civil Rights Movement came into my life" (124)—Walker's political metamorphosis began. Until then she had seen no reason to struggle beyond the effort for daily bread. Ever after, "I have fought and kicked and fasted and prayed and cursed and cried myself to the point of existing. It has been like being born again, literally" (125).

Walker's metamorphosis was surely political in the broad sense, but is it legitimate to call it a culture crossing? At age seventeen a high school girl in rural Georgia fears that the only future open to her is to relive her mother's life of cleaning other people's houses, identifying with the blond heroines of soap operas, and believing that white people are smarter, prettier, and better. At age twenty-three she is sharing a Greenwich Village apartment with the Jewish law student who will become her husband and writing what will turn out to be a prize-winning essay about the Civil Rights Movement. If this is not a culture crossing, what is?

"Part of what existence means to me," Walker wrote in 1966,

> is knowing the difference between what I am now and what I was then. It is being capable of looking after myself intellectually as well as financially. It is being able to tell when I am being wronged and by whom. It means being awake to protect myself and the ones I love. It means being a part of the world community, and being *alert* to which part it is that I have joined, and knowing how to change to

another part if that part does not suit me. To know is to exist: to exist is to be involved, to move about, to see the world with my own eyes. This, at least, the Movement has given me. (125–26)

As Walker dated her metamorphosis by the Civil Rights Movement to an impassioned speech of Martin Luther King, Cherokee leader Wilma Mankiller dated her transformation by the Native American Movement to the 1969 seizure of an island in San Francisco Bay by a group of Native Americans. "The name of the island is Alcatraz. It changed me forever," she wrote in her autobiography *Mankiller: A Chief and Her People.*[33]

Mankiller, whose father was a Cherokee and whose mother "sometimes forgets she is white" (9), lived in a Native American community in Oklahoma until she was almost eleven, when she was unwillingly relocated with her family to San Francisco by the U.S. government. Married at age seventeen and in possession of "two children, a home, and security" by the time of the occupation of Alcatraz, she wrote: "Everyday that passed seemed to give me more self-respect and sense of pride" (193). Calling this period of her life "my awakening," she reported that when the occupation of Alcatraz was over, "I knew for sure that I could no longer remain content as a housewife" (201).

Knowing Rita's story, it is perhaps not surprising to learn that Mankiller's husband—a relatively affluent Ecuadorian who had "not a drop of Indian blood flowing in [his] veins" (146)—objected to her traveling places without him and to the movement meetings she held in their home. Nor does it come as a shock that when he told her she could not have a car, she defied him:

Buying that little red car without my husband's consent or knowledge was my first act of rebellion against a lifestyle that I had come to believe was too narrow and confining for me. I wanted to break free to experience all the changes going on around me—the politics, literature, art, music, and the role of women. But until I bought that little red Mazda, I was unwilling to take any risks to achieve more independence. Once I had the car, I traveled to many tribal events throughout California and even in Oregon and Washington. (202)

Looking back on "those wonderfully sad and crazy years of the 1960s in San Francisco" (157) and recalling that she was "starting to feel restricted by the routine required of a traditional wife" (151),

Mankiller said, "Everything that was happening in the world at that time—Vietnam, peace demonstrations, the civil-rights movement and the seeds of the native-rights movement—had a lasting influence on me. I began to question so many things in my life, including, once again, my marriage" (157). Knowing that she had to make changes, Mankiller enrolled in a junior college. As if once again enacting Willy Russell's script for Rita and Denny, the more independent she learned to be, the more her relationship with her husband deteriorated:

> Hugo could see that I did not fit his mold anymore, but he kept trying. . . . My world was supposed to be within the confines of our home and social life, a world strictly defined by Hugo. But that would no longer do for me. I wanted to set my own limits, and control my destiny. I began to have dreams about more freedom and independence, and I finally came to understand that I did not have to live a life based on someone else's dreams. (158–59)

Quite evidently, Mankiller's process of leaving her housewife self behind began several years before the seizure of Alcatraz. It was the occupation, however, that determined the direction of her culture crossing. Indeed, it is fair to say that from 1966 or so she started moving out of the traditional wife/mother culture she inhabited, albeit with no clear destination in mind. Only after November 1969 did she head back to the Cherokee culture that she had known as a child. By the time she arrived there she was not simply the Cherokee woman she proudly calls herself. She was a Native American activist.

REPLACEMENT AND COEXISTENCE

Call life a chronology of changes or a series of educational metamorphoses. Either way, these are culture crossings as well as personal transformations and since every single one of us makes a number of these journeys, we can all be said to be multiply cultured people. Once the varieties of metamorphoses are recognized it becomes clear, moreover, that a linear model according to which the end state of one educational metamorphosis erases and replaces the end state of a previous one does not do justice to all the facts. To be sure, it seems to fit Malcolm's case. But not all whole person transformations conform to it.

Think of Rosamund. At the start of Drabble's novel she is a literary scholar who spends her days tutoring students and working in the British Museum on a thesis about Elizabethan sonnet sequences. Drabble does not tell us how her heroine became such a person, but one may suppose that in so doing she underwent an educational metamorphosis. According to a model in which each new metamorphosis replaces the outcome of its predecessor, Rosamund's scholarly self would have vanished after Octavia's birth. Yet this is not what happens. Some women who are transformed by mothering have been known to shed their scholarly selves as snakes do their skins. But although Rosamund undergoes a whole person metamorphosis after her baby is born, her scholarly self survives this change. In quick succession Rosamund completes her dissertation, accepts invitations to write articles in her chosen field, finds it gratifying that she will in the future be addressed as Dr. Rosamund Stacey, and starts thinking about turning her attention to eighteenth-century literary topics.

"My story suggests that education is not, in fact, transformation. It is not subtraction. Education is addition. As such, education sets up a dialogue among past, present, and possible selves," insisted an academic born into a working-class household.[34] Rosamund's story suggests that education can involve addition, subtraction, and transformation more or less simultaneously. Insofar as her old carefree self turns into a new, very different person, hers is an instance of transformation. It is also a case of subtraction in that the new person who is the outcome of Rosamund's mothering metamorphosis replaces that carefree young woman self. And it is an example of addition because after Rosamund's mothering metamorphosis occurs, the new person who emerges lives side by side with her older scholarly self.

It is of course true that Rosamund's mothering self might eventually produce changes in her scholarly self or even remove it from the scene. Initially, however, these two selves seem satisfied to operate in separate, distinct contexts while living comfortably side by side with little if any interaction. In her relations with Octavia Rosamund talks, acts, and sees the world in accordance with the mothering metamorphosis she has just undergone, whereas in her relations with her students and colleagues she talks, acts, and sees the world more or less as her scholarly self always has.

Rosamund's fictional experience has its counterparts in the nonfictional world. Thus, for example, in a memoir about growing up Puerto Rican in New York, Esmeralda Santiago reported being accustomed to disengaging Negi, her Puerto Rican self, from Esmeralda, her New York self.[35] When as an adult she fell in love, she then learned to disengage both of these from Chiquita, the ultrafeminine self she became in her relationship with her "Turkish lover."[36]

Yet just as alienation looms large in cases of replacement, the conflicts generated by the clash of selves in cases of coexistence must be reckoned with. It is standard practice to view dual and multiple roles as sources of ambivalence and conflict. When, however, educational metamorphoses occur, the conflicts run deep, for they are between the different selves or identities that result from crossings into different cultures.

Bartky, for instance, spoke of her feminist consciousness as being "radically alienated from her world and often divided against herself" (21). In Harrington's study, a woman lawyer reported that after the birth of her first child she began having trouble being both an adversary and a mother: "She could not be aggressive and competitive for eight or nine or ten hours a day and then, on her return home, become loving, sympathetic, patient, and generous" (146). Guinier admitted, "Even my own mother complained that sometimes I cross-examined her."[37] A young African American who as a scholarship boy at a predominantly white prep school learned to flip back and forth between an angry, cursing "street" self and a sophisticated "professional" self intimated that by the time he entered college it had become increasingly distasteful to do so.[38]

Even when the final outcome of an educational metamorphosis is the replacement of one self by the next, the new self can conflict with the old self during the process of change. Thus, Mark Mathabane wrote that while going back and forth between home and the white ranch where he perfected his tennis game, he developed a dual personality. At first he could switch from one to another as the situation warranted. "Gradually, however, like Jekyll and Hyde, one personality began to predominate. I could no longer pretend, fawn or wear the mask of servility, without my true self violently rebelling. I knew that I had to find a safe way to be myself without breaking the law, or else I would surely go mad" (241–42).

Moreover, an old self can send residual messages after a transformation has occurred. "My old self doesn't respect my new self. My old self says I'm living a lazy, overprivileged life. My new self says, what more could I do? My old self says, you're not doing anything productive. My new self says, you don't know how to think," one enactor of the American Dream reported.[39]

In *The Souls of Black Folk*, African-American philosopher and social theorist W. E. B. Dubois wrote that a black person in America—the term he used was "Negro"—is gifted with "second sight" or "a double-consciousness" in that he sees himself through the eyes of others. In the course of elaborating this insight he added another to his analysis: "One ever feels his twoness,—an American, a Negro; two souls, two thoughts, two unreconciled strivings; two warring ideals in one dark body."[40] When DuBois's concept of "feeling one's twoness" is expanded to threeness and beyond, it bears on the idea of educational metamorphoses. The body does not have to be dark—nor, as some might hypothesize, female—for an individual to experience the warring of ideals or the conflict between traits or dispositions. Nor need there be only two selves living together in a single body.[41] On the other hand, the existence of multiple selves or identities does not necessarily mean that they will be in conflict.

Can an aggressive lawyer self live comfortably with a compassionate mother self? Can a marine sniper self remain a loving son self? Can an academically educated self get along with an earlier working-class self? Some kinds of people may be better able than others to accommodate potentially dueling identities, some selves may be so different from others that they cannot live together peaceably, and some selves may be less apt to create conflict and pain than others. "Here, on paper, I can be in two worlds and control them both," wrote one scholar with a working-class background.[42] On the other hand, a working-class woman who became a novelist concluded, "For some working class people the secrets are all they have. Thus, writing about them feels like betrayal."[43]

Look at an individual life from a temporal perspective and one sees a succession of personal transformations. Since each one of these is also a culture crossing, one may say that just as many contemporary societies are cultural mixes, so are individual human beings. Look at a temporal slice or cross section of an individual life and one is likely to see two or more identities living peaceably together—or perhaps not. Either way, because every individual may be made up of coexisting selves and every self represents a culture crossing, he or she can be considered a multiply cultured creature. In effect, we human beings are multiply cultured in two respects. Not only do we cross from one culture into the next in the course of our lives. At any given time we are also likely to be inhabited by coexisting selves representing different cultures.

NOTES

1. Margaret Drabble, "With All My Love, (Signed) Mama," in *Motherhood*, ed. Susan Cahill (New York: Avon, 1982), 6.

2. Adrienne Rich, *Of Woman Born* (New York: Bantam Books, 1977), 223.

3. Margaret Drabble, *Thank You All Very Much* (New York: New American Library, 1965), 143. Page references to this book, originally called *The Milestone*, are in parentheses in the text.

4. Simone de Beauvoir, *The Second Sex* (New York: Bantam Books, 1961), 484. For further discussion of the dangers for women that attach to metamorphoses like Rosamund's, see Rich, *Of Woman Born*.

5. Shulamith Firestone, *The Dialectic of Sex* (New York: Bantam Books, 1971), 73.

6. Jeffner Allen, "Motherhood: The Annihilation of Women," in *Mothering*, ed. Joyce Trebilcot (Totowa, NJ: Rowman and Allenheld, 1984), 316.

7. Susan Maushart, *The Mask of Motherhood* (New York: Penguin Books, 2000), 4.

8. Maushart, 245.

9. Ann Oakley, *Becoming a Mother* (Oxford: Martin Robertson and Co., 1979), 263.

10. Why then speak of a *mothering* metamorphosis? Why not call Rosamund's a *parenting* one? More men today than perhaps ever before are shouldering or sharing the role of primary caretaker of young children with women. As even greater numbers participate fully in the rearing of newborns, it may well make sense to adopt a gender-neutral label for the metamorphosis in question. So long as many, many more women than men engage in this practice, however, the gender-neutral label "parenting metamorphosis" is deeply misleading. For even though some males undergo a mothering metamorphosis, the cultural relations and activities that give rise to this kind of educational transformation have historically been and still are strongly associated with women. See Susan

Rae Peterson, "Against 'Parenting,'" in Trebilcot, *Mothering*, 62–69, for a detailed analysis of this issue. In light of the fear that motherhood annihilates women, is it not advisable to disregard the facts and eschew the gendered label? Insofar as the parenting label conceals the degree to which both the metamorphosis at issue and the related cultural practices are associated primarily with women, it is doubtful that its use will further goals such as the equality of women. On the contrary, a knowledge of just what the metamorphosis involves, an appreciation of how it affects women, and an understanding of whether it contributes to women's oppression would seem to be far more conducive to creating "a subjectivity and a world that is open and free" (Jeffner Allen, "Motherhood: The Annihilation of Women," 314).

11. See, e.g., Samuel Hynes, *The Growing Season* (New York: Viking, 2003), 6; William Woodruff, *Beyond Nab End* (London: Abacus, 2003), 407.

12. Mark Mathabane, *Kaffir Boy* (New York: Simon and Schuster, 1986), 28.

13. Robert K. Fullinwider, "Multicultural Education," in *A Companion to the Philosophy of Education*, ed. Randall Curren (Malden, MA: Blackwell Publishing, 2003), 490.

14. This is the title of part III of his book.

15. Helen Horowitz, *Alma Mater* (Boston: Beacon Press, 1984), 167.

16. Emlyn Williams, *George: An Early Autobiography* (New York: Random House, 1961), 295.

17. Frank's insight also apparently holds good for the field of classical music conducting. "Ms. Alsop has given much thought to the issue of gender and conducting. She has shaped her style to avoid being seen as too feminine. She trained herself, for instance, to look squarely at the brass players when calling for a big outburst; she said she had previously tended to 'apologize' by looking away." Daniel J. Wakin, "Best Wishes on Your Job. Now Get Out," *New York Times*, October 9, 2005, AR31.

18. Mona Harrington, *Women Lawyers* (New York: Plume Books, 1995), 48. Page references are in parentheses in the text.

19. Lani Guinier, "Models and Mentors," in *Becoming Gentlemen*, ed. Lani Guinier, Michelle Fine, and Jane Balin (Boston: Beacon Press, 1997), 99.

20. Lani Guinier, Michelle Fine, and Jane Balin, *Becoming Gentlemen* (Boston: Beacon Press, 1997). Page references are in parentheses in the text.

21. Guinier, "Models and Mentors," 85.

22. Guinier, "Models and Mentors," 85.

23. It needs to be stressed here that men of color and men from working-class backgrounds make similar culture crossings and undergo similar metamorphoses in law school.

24. Anthony Swofford, *Jarhead* (New York: Scribner, 2003), 248. Page references are in parentheses in the text. Referring to the death three years

earlier of her four-year-old daughter, a mother said, "It becomes part of who you are. . . . You can't possibly be the same person you were before. It's like these young men who go off to war and they come back different. They're not innocent anymore. You know such deep, deep pain exists, and it brings you to this whole different level of humanness." Bella English, "Life after Lulu," *Boston Globe*, June 10, 2004, D5.

25. Karen Houppert, "Military Recruiters Are Now Targeting Sixth Graders. Who's Next?" *The Nation*, September 12, 2005, 20.

26. William James, "The Moral Equivalent of War," in *Philosophical Perspectives on Peace*, ed. Howard P. Kainz (Athens: Ohio University Press, 1987), 213–25.

27. For descriptions of very different military metamorphoses see David Lipsky, *Absolutely American: Four Years at West Point* (Boston: Houghton Mifflin, 2003). But cf. Tony Perry, "For Marine Snipers, War Is Up Close and Personal," *Boston Globe*, April 19, 2004, A10; John J. Lumpkin, "Marine General Says It's 'Fun' to Shoot Some in Combat," *Boston Globe*, February 2, 2005, A4.

28. J. Glenn Gray, *The Warriors* (New York: Harper and Row, 1970), 9.

29. Howard Zinn, *You Can't Get Off a Moving Train* (Boston: Beacon Press, 1994), 98.

30. Sandra Bartky, *Femininity and Domination* (New York: Routledge, 1990), chap. 1. Page references are in parentheses in the text.

31. Bartky herself says that the experience she describes "goes far beyond that sphere of human activity we regard ordinarily as 'political'" (11).

32. Alice Walker, *In Search of Our Mothers' Gardens* (New York: Harcourt Brace & Company, 1983), 122. Page references are in parentheses in the text.

33. Wilma Mankiller, *Mankiller* (New York: St. Martin's Press, 1993), 163. Page references are in parentheses in the text.

34. Donna Burns Phillips, "Past Voices, Present Speakers," in *This Fine Place So Far from Home*, ed. C. L. Barney Dews and Carolyn Leste Law (Philadelphia: Temple University Press, 1993), 230.

35. Esmeralda Santiago, *Almost a Woman* (New York: Vintage, 1998), 155.

36. Esmeralda Santiago, *The Turkish Lover* (New York: Da Capo Press, 2004), 209.

37. Guinier, "Models and Mentors," 88.

38. Irene Sege, "Student of Change," *Boston Globe*, October 19, 2005, F8.

39. Renny Christopher, "A Carpenter's Daughter," in Dews and Law, *This Fine Place*, 140.

40. W. E. B. DuBois, "The Souls of Black Folk," in *Three Negro Classics* (New York: Avon Books, 1965), 215.

41. "The two-souls paradigm is essentially reductive, for even a man as unremarkable as myself must have more than two souls." Wilson J. Moses, "Ambivalent Maybe," in Dews and Law, *This Fine Place*, 187.

42. Laurel Johnson Black, "Stupid Rich Bastards," in Dews and Law, *This Fine Place*, 24.

43. Valerie Miner, "Writing and Teaching with Class," in *Working-Class Women in the Academy*, ed. Michelle M. Tokarczyk and Elizabeth A. Fay (Amherst: University of Massachusetts Press, 1993), 77.

6

Circulating the Gift of Education

SOME PAINS OF ASSIMILATIONISM

In Ovid's rendition of the Pygmalion myth the question of what, if anything, Galatea's metamorphosis from an ivory statue into a living, breathing woman costs her does not arise. Telling his story from the sculptor's point of view, he gives Galatea no chance to express her feelings. The truth is, however, that even educational metamorphoses that almost everyone would agree are improvements often exact a heavy toll.

It goes without saying that whole person or identity transformations can yield pleasure. For all her worry, Rosamund's is marked by moments of sheer delight. Schaller reported Ildefonso's joy at discovering language as well as his growing grief as he began to realize what he had been missing for well nigh twenty-seven years. Malcolm described the exhilaration he experienced first as a reader and then as a prison debater as well as his shock at reading about slavery and also the actions of the British in India. And when, in *The Corn Is Green*, Miss Moffatt reminds her student that he might fail the entrance examination to Oxford he says:

> Don't speak about it. . . . I have *been* to Oxford, and . . . I have come back—from the world! Since the day I was born, I have been a prisoner behind a stone wall, and now somebody has given me a leg-up

to have a look at the other side . . . they cannot drag me back again,
they cannot, they *must* give me a push and send me over! (70–71)

In addition, traits often disappear in the course of an educational
metamorphosis that will not be missed. Think of Malcolm's desire
to pimp or Rodriguez's shyness with Gringos.

Nevertheless, our case studies are filled with reports of pain and
suffering. Sounding just like the nineteenth-century immigrants
who portrayed themselves as being "between two worlds," Rita
tells Frank that she feels like a freak. She is not alone. Recalling the
period when she traveled back and forth between her academic
high school and the housing project where she and her family
lived, African American lawyer Janet McDonald described a similar experience: "I was straddling contradictory worlds and not fitting in anywhere."[1] Remarking that upward mobility "is the
essence of the American Dream," an academic woman from a
working-class background described herself as "unprepared for
the marginality and estrangement I would feel as my 'dream' came
true."[2] She and others like her, she said, "saw ourselves as living on
the margins of two cultural worlds but as members of neither."[3]
Another called herself "a stranger in a strange land."[4] Someone
else wrote, "To the outside world you may look middle-class, but
you know your birthmarks."[5]

Feeling marginal is one common complaint of those who undergo educational metamorphoses, and experiencing loss is another. "I will never stop being disadvantaged as long as that familiar pain remains centered in my chest, the pain that has come from
so much dislocation, separation, and loss," wrote a woman from a
working-class background earning a Ph.D. in American literature.[6]
Granted, when a person divests him or herself of earlier outmoded
or now dysfunctional cultural stock the toll exacted by an educational metamorphosis will actually be a boon. But the price is just
as apt to be an entire way of life.

The educational metamorphosis of Mexican American Richard
Rodriguez could not have been more successful; indeed, he seems
to have achieved the American Dream of bettering oneself through
education. Yet his memoir is notable primarily as a narrative of
loss. In the process of turning into a well-educated American he
lost his fluency in Spanish, and that was the least of it. As soon as

English became the language of the Rodriguez family, the special feeling of closeness at home was diminished. Furthermore, as Richard's days were devoted to understanding the meaning of words, it became difficult for him to hear intimate family voices. When his home was Spanish speaking, it was a noisy, playful, warm, emotionally charged environment; with the advent of English the atmosphere became quiet and restrained. There was no acrimony. The family remained loving. But the experience of "feeling individualized" by family members was now rare, and occasions for intimacy were infrequent.

Rodriguez's variation on the Pygmalion myth is a story of alienation: from his parents, for whom he soon had no names; from the Spanish language, in which he lost his childhood fluency; from his Mexican roots, in which he showed no interest; from his feelings and emotions, which all but disappeared as he learned to control them; from his body itself, as he discovered when he took a construction job after his senior year in college. And his tale has many echoes.

Recalling her undergraduate experience at Harvard, Elaine Mar confessed, "Over four years the distance between Denver and Cambridge had grown until I was as far away as another country. My parents weren't able to visit. Like my grandfather, I'd immigrated with no way to send for my family."[7] A sociology professor from a working-class family wrote, "I know the world in which my parents live and work. But they have no similar knowledge of, nor even access to, my world."[8] According to another academic, her trouble was "a perceived gulf between my life and the lives of those I love and have left behind."[9] In her memoir about growing up Puerto Rican in New York City, Harvard graduate Esmeralda Santiago said, "Every day we spent in Brooklyn was like a curtain dropping between me and my other life."[10] In a later volume she called her loss, "a Puerto Rican afternoon humming with bees, the proud cackle of a hen with chicks, the sudden, loud thunder and pounding rain of a tropical squall."[11]

Marginality and loss are the two sides of the single coin—assimilation. To feel that one fits into or belongs to a given cultural entity—it does not matter if it is academia, Wimpole Street society, a Michigan public school, or the U.S. Marine Corps—one needs to be, or at least feel, accepted. For those nineteenth-century immigrants to the

U.S., acceptance was a function of the degree to which they became assimilated into mainstream U.S. culture, and assimilation appears to be the issue for our culture crossers, be they immigrants in the first dictionary sense or not. Unfortunately, by its very nature the process that is considered necessary for fitting in entails loss.

Because many different terms are used to designate what is here being called "assimilation," students of immigration have sometimes represented this process by the formula $A + B = A$, where the letter A stands for a host culture and the letter B for culture crossers.[12] This equation reflects the fact that assimilation is a one-way affair: a crosser changes so as to fit into a culture; the culture does not change so as to accommodate the crosser.

From the standpoint of a culture, $A + B = A$ is a process in which a culture crosser acquires the stock—the ways of thinking, modes of behavior, and so on—that the culture standardly transmits to its own members; and at the same time disposes of whatever tell-tale stock signifies membership in his or her former culture. The culture into which the crosser moves does not in its turn add stock in the crosser's possession to its own portfolio, nor does it divest itself of stock that the crosser finds difficult to appropriate. The culture crosser is thus presented with two interconnected problems. He or she has to acquire stock belonging to the new culture—something that can be difficult, even painful to accomplish; and also give up stock belonging to the old culture—something that can be equally hard to do.

Since assimilation is a matter of degree, it is to be expected that one culture crosser will end up being more assimilated than another into a given cultural entity. It need hardly be added that assimilation can also be more difficult for one person to achieve than another. When, for example, being white or male or upper middle class or Christian or heterosexual is a culture's defining characteristic, an African American or woman or working-class person or Muslim or Jew or gay or lesbian is likely to find it harder to feel accepted than does someone who possesses the desired characteristic.

It is also to be expected that even relatively well-assimilated new arrivals are apt to retain some of the behaviors and some of the likes and dislikes that were passed down to them by their culture of departure. But then, if enough culture crossers are assimilated into a culture, its portfolio of stock is likely to undergo some degree of change. In light of this, the formula $A + B = A'$, where A' stands for some slight modification of the host culture, is perhaps a more accurate rendition of the realities of assimilation than $A + B = A$. The latter equation does, however, represent the hoped-for result of assimilation.

The pressure exerted by assimilation contributes to the marginality and loss experienced by those who undergo educational metamorphoses, and also helps to explain why betrayal is a common theme in our case studies. In Shaw's play the only person who exhibits jealousy and feels betrayed by Eliza is Henry Higgins, and this is because she no longer wishes to be under his thumb. Rita's plight is more typical. When Frank asks her why she never became a "proper student" she says:

> Rita: See, if I'd started takin' school seriously, I would have had to become different from me mates, an' that's not allowed.
>
> Frank: By whom?
>
> Rita: By your mates, by your family, by everyone. (17)

"Why can't he just let me get on with me learnin'?" she says of her husband. "You'd think I was havin' a bloody affair the way he behaves" (32).

Once Rita's husband learns that she is still on the birth control pill, he stops wondering where the girl he married has gone and burns her books. When even this outrage does not deter her from reading Chekhov's plays and writing essays on *Macbeth* and *Peer Gynt*, Denny packs her suitcase. "He said either I stop comin' here an' come off the pill or I could get out altogether," Rita reports (46). "It was an ultimatum. I explained to him. I didn't get narced or anythin'. I just explained to him how I had to do this. He said it's warped me. He said I'd betrayed him. I suppose I have" (46–47).

In its intensity and danger Rita's experience does not come close to matching Mark's. When Mrs. Smith gave him the tennis racket, the game was considered in South Africa, as in many other late-twentieth-century societies, to be a white person's sport. As Mark devoted more and more time to tennis and began entering black tournaments, a black player helped him land a job on a white tennis ranch where he was allowed to do the unheard of: practice with and play against whites. Ironically, the better tennis he played, the more his father and others taunted him for "trying to become an imitation white man by playing this silly thing called tennis" (216).

It is not surprising that white people condemned Mark for overstepping himself. But many black people "interpreted my love for the English language, for poetry, for tennis, as a sign that I was trying to be white" (255). Because of his participation in the "white" sport of tennis they "mistook me for an Uncle Tom" (xi). A few black youngsters "saw me as someone worth emulating," he says, but the hatred and jealousy of others "were implacable. These continued to call me an Uncle Tom, and to threaten me with death" (240).

The experiences of Mark and Rita are repeated across nations, classes, races, ethnicities, and genders. Esmeralda Santiago confronted hatred, jealousy, and feelings of betrayal from the moment her junior high school guidance counselor announced over the loudspeaker with great pride that she was applying to the High School of Performing Arts—a public New York City institution requiring an entrance examination. That very day Lulu, the leader of a girls' gang, told her "You think you're better than us? Well, you're just a spick, and don't you forget it,"[13] and then proceeded to spit in Esmeralda's face. When the guidance counselor announced Esmeralda's acceptance at the prestigious high school, Lulu and her friends stopped the threats and insults and beat Esmeralda up.[14]

Upon leaving Erasmus Hall High School for Vassar College, Janet McDonald chastised herself "for having abandoned my suffering tribe to learn tennis and philosophy with children of privilege."[15] Accusing herself of betrayal, Lorene Cary, an African-American girl from Philadelphia who attended an elite New England boarding school, reported feeling "traitorous" when she graduated.[16] Even after teaching at St. Paul's and subsequently becoming a trustee, she caught herself watching the first black teacher at the school and trying "to deduce from his gait and the way he inclined his head whether the small man with the tiny eyes was a traitor or an advocate."[17] And a white woman from a working-class background who taught women's studies at a U.S. university in her turn recorded a recurring dream: "Although the details change, my dreams generally portray my inability to feel at home in middle-class environments and my fear of betraying working-class friends."[18]

It is commonplace that learning is hard work, hence intrinsically painful. Let it therefore be noted that the pain and suffering reported in case studies of educational metamorphoses are not intrinsic to the act or process of learning. They follow from the assumption of assimilationism and the fact that these personal transformations are also culture crossings. If Rita's educational metamorphosis were nothing but a whole person transformation, her husband might not like her new identity, but he would not accuse her of betrayal. In his eyes the problem is not just that Rita is walking, talking, and behaving differently. Her new walk, talk, and behavior signify her assimilation into a culture whose members Denny at once envies and distrusts. Similarly, the young Esmeralda Santiago was not simply in the process of becoming someone her schoolmates did not know. She was moving into a culture they feared and resented.

CAN A PERSON GO HOME AFTER AN EDUCATIONAL METAMORPHOSIS?

It is not likely that Galatea will feel anxiety over having betrayed someone or entertain thoughts of going home again. A woman who used to be a statue has left behind no family members or friends. There is no culture to which she once belonged. In the minds of the people in our case studies, however, the idea of returning or not returning home looms large. Indeed, even though Minik had no immediate family to go back to, when as a teenager he became disillusioned, he told a friend that he would kill himself if he could not go home. For *home* is an elastic term that can be used to refer to nations, cultures, and geographical locations as well as to "private" homes.[19]

An English professor with a working-class background was thinking of his "private" home when he wrote: "Although I hesitate to admit it, I must tell you that the only time my parents and I and my brother and sister have been together since I left home was for my parents' silver wedding anniversary. I suspect the next occasion will be a funeral."[20] The home Minik had in mind was, in contrast, the Polar North culture. And when a specialist in Latin American history wrote, "My lifestyle may be middle class, but my heart and soul are Latina and working class,"[21] she was in effect saying that although she had been transformed into an academic, returning to her cultural home presented no problems.

Admittedly, some people do not want to go back home and others would like to return home but cannot because home has disappeared. But people's desires and intentions aside, when an educational metamorphosis has occurred, talk about going home is apt to be ambiguous. When Eliza bemoans that she cannot go back to her flower basket, is she saying that she is unable to revert to her former self or that her new self cannot bear to return to the culture in which her flower girl self lived? Did Minik plan to go back to the culture of the Polar North as the American young man he had become, or did he expect on his arrival there to shed his new identity and revert back to the old one?

As if to prove that when education transforms a person one never knows what will happen next, Minik's new world fell apart soon after his relatively easy crossing into American culture. In 1901, his foster father was accused of misappropriating museum funds and soon thereafter the New York Museum of Natural History withdrew the financial support it had been giving Wallace. Three years later Mrs. Wallace died. Then to top things off, Minik discovered that the funeral the museum had arranged for his father had been a charade. To satisfy the young boy, it had staged a fake ceremony in which an imitation body was placed on the ground and stones put on top of it. In fact, as Minik's schoolmates informed him some time later, his father's body had already been chopped up and the bones placed in the museum's collection. "After that," said Wallace, "he was never the same boy" (96).

Before Minik lost faith in American culture, he rejected the very thought of returning north. Nevertheless, in August 1909, Minik found himself once again in the Arctic. There, welcoming cousins taught him the language he had completely forgotten and the skills and knowledge he now needed and had not acquired as a child. But although Minik was a quick learner, he did not become a happy man.

The returning Minik appears to have been attempting to revert to his earlier self—or rather, to an adult version of the same. If Galatea were to go back to being a statue after giving birth to Paphos, she would not be able to recall the human culture in which she had lived. But Minik was no Galatea. The earlier identity he approximated did not replace his newer American self. Instead, the latter lived on and was forever reminding his Inuit self of its existence.

At the height of his disillusionment with America Minik said:

> These are the civilized men who steal, and murder, and torture, and pray and say "Science." My poor people don't know that the meteorite that they used till Peary took it fell off a star. But they know that the hungry must be fed, and cold men warmed, and helpless people cared for, and they do it. (133)

Ultimately, however, he became someone Mill could have cited in defense of his oft-challenged thesis that a person who has experienced what Mill considered to be the "higher" pleasures associated with Socrates and the "lower" ones associated with the fool or the pig will prefer the "higher."

"Was I satisfied with the crude life there?" Minik asked rhetorically upon his return to New York seven years after his departure for the north. "Yes and no. The climate suited me and my health was better than when here. But the hard dreary life of the people and the conditions under which they live are very monotonous to one who knows of the high state of civilization" (209). "It would have been better for me," he added, "had I never been brought to civilization and educated. It leaves me between two extremes where it would seem that I can get nowhere. . . . It's like rotting in a cellar to go there after living in a civilized country" (209).

There is no way of knowing if Minik would have felt that he belonged in America the second time round. Just as he had longed for New York when he arrived back home, when he was once more in New York he longed for home. But in 1917 he found a job he liked in a lumber camp, and when spring and the mud season arrived a new friend offered him work on a family farm. For a second time Minik was taken into an American home and made to feel part of the family. The first happy period of his adult life did not last long, however, for by then it was 1918 and the flu epidemic was at its height. In late October Minik caught influenza. Seven days later he died of the bronchial pneumonia that followed.

Had Minik simply gone back to the Polar North for a brief stay he might have been able to switch back and forth between identities with ease. A U.S. professor reported that on every visit home her mother tells her she hasn't changed at all: "She means this as, and I take it as, a compliment—though, of course, it's not entirely true. I have changed."[22] On a rather different note, some young men who have been transformed from relatively peaceful individuals into terrorists seem able to revert back to the selves they once were as the occasion demands. And, of course, Nazi officers in Hitler's Germany have often been portrayed as switching back and forth between their old congenial family selves and their newer monstrous selves.

Although reverting even temporarily to the person one once was can make it easier to go back home, it is not always an option. A man from a southern U.S. rural working-class background confesses, "I can't get rid of the contamination of the academy. I can't put the genie back into the bottle."[23] Calling himself "a working-class academic," a man raised in Wisconsin said, "By sloughing off our working-class skins, we make it through college and become teachers."[24]

In stark contrast to Minik, who returned home as his former self grown up, Heidi Bud, the subject of the documentary film *Daughter of Danang*,[25] went back to Vietnam as the new person she had become in the United States. Indeed, her culture crossing so Americanized her that one wonders if she could possibly have reverted to her former self had she tried.

In 1975 a six-year-old girl whose Vietnamese name was Hiep arrived in San Francisco under the auspices of the U.S. government sponsored "Orphan Airlift." Although the single American woman who adopted her did not know this, Hiep was not an orphan. Her mother had given her up to an American social worker in the program in the belief that her daughter, who was of mixed parentage, would be in danger if she remained in Vietnam: "If you had worked for Americans and had racially mixed children, they said those kids would be gathered up, they would be soaked in gasoline and burnt" she said many years later (1).

Upon the child's arrival in the United States a Vietnamese journalist told Hiep and the children with whom she had traveled, "You don't understand what's going on now, but this is very important. You have to remember who you are" (2). Believing that her new daughter had no reason to remember, Ann Neville brought up the girl she renamed Heidi to be "101% American." As Heidi permed her hair in her Tennessee home before she went to school; as she ate bologna and told people that she was born in South Carolina; as she forgot her home, her family, and the Vietnamese language; and as the acquired characteristics that at the very beginning of her life had turned her into a little Vietnamese girl were replaced by skills, traits, and dispositions belonging to her new culture: an American is what she became.

Twenty-two years later this "white Southerner," as Heidi thought of herself, returned to Vietnam to meet her biological mother who had been tracked down just four months before. Accompanying Heidi were two filmmakers who had heard about the upcoming reunion and wanted to capture "what we believed would be a re-connection by Heidi with her long forgotten Vietnamese roots" (1). Everyone—Heidi, her biological family, and the filmmakers—expected the reunion to be "a healing story, a kind of full-circle coming home" (2). Instead, *Daughter of Danang* is a cautionary tale about going home as one's new self. The documentary leaves little doubt that Heidi brought American style love to spare to her homecoming and that her birth family was overjoyed to see her again. But no amount of love and joy could bridge the gap between Heidi's assumptions about a daughter's familial duties and theirs. This woman with a 101 percent American identity could not fathom the Vietnamese expectation that she shoulder her share of the responsibility for her mother's upkeep and care. Her kin with their 101 percent Vietnamese identities could not fathom her American reluctance to do so.[26]

GOING HOME BEARING GIFTS

Shortly before Minik returned to the north he was thinking about organizing an expedition to the Pole. Having read extensively about the Arctic, he had come to believe that the standard approach could not work and that he had a better plan. One college president was so impressed with Minik's idea that he promised him free tuition to pursue a bachelor's degree in science. Said

Minik's sponsor: "I have known Minik only a few days, but have every confidence in him. I do not think it too much to say that he may be a veritable Moses among his people" (126). Telling people that he felt like a freak in college and soon dropping out, Minik apparently saw things differently.

Malcolm X, not Minik, is the person in our case studies who became a Moses-like figure. One of the most striking features of his transformation from hoodlum to a leader of black Americans is that he wanted to go back to Harlem. He had no desire to return to his former self, however; no wish whatsoever to be a pimp and drug dealer in the culture he had left behind. And so he returned in the very capacities that Minik had earlier rejected, namely those of missionary and teacher.

Wilma Mankiller's variation on the Pygmalion myth is very different from Malcolm's, but with respect to going home it too is a success story. Returning to Oklahoma as her new self initially for a brief visit and then with the intention to stay, she ultimately gave her tribe seventeen years of service. "When we first moved back," she recalled,

> I felt as though folks welcomed us, but for a while, they seemed to treat us more like company than family. Little by little, they warmed up. I suppose they finally saw that we meant to stay put. I recall the day I knew I was really and truly home. . . . I spied some old Cherokee men sitting on the benches. They were chewing tobacco and talking over the world's most important problems, just as old Cherokee men have done in Stilwell for a long, long time. As I walked by them, I heard one of them say to the others, 'There goes John Mankiller's granddaughter.'" (216)

Soon thereafter Mankiller began work for the Cherokee Nation of Oklahoma in a low-level management position. In that job and in her subsequent work for the tribe she devoted herself to helping her people "figure out how to live successfully in a very modern, fast-paced world, while preserving our cultural values and tradition" (254). Remarkably, given the overwhelming odds against her—a devastating automobile accident, a form of muscular dystrophy that can lead to paralysis, and the fact that no woman had ever led a major Indian tribe—she eventually rose to be principal chief of the Cherokee Nation.

Ildefonso's journey home is another success story. Some months after he took a welding job at a shipyard, Schaller met him and his brother Mario, who was also born deaf. Ildefonso mimed to Mario and translated to Schaller in sign language, all the while telling her that he could no longer gesture and mime with his brother the way he used to because he had learned too much ASL. But although Ildefonso's fluency in miming was somewhat diminished, he was able to forge a new role for his new self within the small culture of languageless men.

According to Schaller,

Ildefonso's manners were serious and business-like. He was the ringmaster, keeping the rhythm, keeping the show moving. His eyes leaped back and forth from my eyes to the storytellers, measuring my response and their performance. . . . He wanted me to know who he had been, how he had lived, and his only experience with tribal life, with community. He knew who he was now and knew that what he had learned could not be appreciated without knowledge of where he had started. "Look! Look! See! Do you see? It's so different, so different, completely different," he signed again and again. He looked at his friends, who stared back at him across the mysterious gulf that he had managed to cross. (188)

Schaller's description brings to mind Plato's cave allegory. In the *Republic*, Socrates imagines a cave inhabited by people who remain in one place and can only see straight ahead because their necks and legs are in fetters. These men and women are utterly deceived. They believe they possess knowledge, whereas in actual fact they have none at all: in the cave they see the mere shadows of things, not the objects themselves. Socrates calls education the art of turning around.[27] In the cave allegory only some men and women are freed from their fetters so that they can turn and see the light.

Socrates asks what will become of those who leave the cave and claim an education. He anticipates that they will wish to contemplate the knowledge they gain forever, but says that they must not be allowed this luxury. They do not have to return to the cave indefinitely, but because the educated few now possess the most basic and important knowledge there is, they have an obligation to go back down at least for a while and govern those they left behind. Although Ildefonso cannot be said to have become the ruler of the languageless men he left behind, when he became a speaker of American Sign Language (ASL) he did something equally important. He became their interpreter of the larger society and a translator of their culture for people like Schaller.

The one exception Socrates made to the special form of going home he envisioned for the people who leave the cave and become "enlightened" is that those who have gained knowledge of their own accord and against the will of the government need not return to the cave. His reason was that they have no debt to repay. Had he had access to our case studies he might have judged that Yentl belongs in this category. After all, she becomes a Torah scholar of her own accord and against the will of the governors of her community. He might conceivably have included Malcolm's self-education in this group too. But he would not have waived the debt for Ildefonso, let alone for all those for whom school and university have been significant educational agents.

Think of Richard Rodriguez. He did not grow into a literary scholar of his own accord. In his own words, he was "groomed for a position in the multiuniversity's leadership class" (151) by the California parochial school system and the public and private universities he then attended. To Socrates' way of thinking, he therefore ought to have given something back to those with less formal education than he. To be sure, Rodriguez did not ask for and has said that he did not want or need the affirmative action rewards that were showered upon him. However, the benefits that Socrates would say Rodriguez reaped did not just accrue from those measures. "The great lesson of school," wrote Rodriguez, was "that I had a public identity. Fortunately, my teachers were unsentimental about their responsibility. What they understood was that I needed to speak a public language" (19).

In Shaw's variation on the Pygmalion story, Colonel Pickering wonders if Professor Higgins has the right to transform Eliza Doolittle without her consent. Others have asked the same question about Itard's experiment on Victor. The cave allegory suggests that questions can be asked about the other side of the educational equation: for instance, Does the person who undergoes an educational metamorphosis have a responsibility to pay back what has been received? If so, to whom and in what coin of the realm?

As Schaller gave Ildefonso ASL that in his case was the gift of language itself, school gave Rodriguez English that for him was the gift of inclusion in public life. We usually think of gifts as things exchanged between two parties. However, the kind of repayment Socrates envisions does not require that Rodriguez give back something directly. Although he may not have been thinking of what anthropologists call "gift exchange," his idea is reminiscent of that practice as described by Lewis Hyde.

In gift exchange, "Whatever we have been given is supposed to be given away again, not kept. Or, if it is kept, something of similar value shall move in its stead."[28] The gift always moves, and it does so in a circle. You may of course keep the present someone gives you. It ceases to be a gift, however, unless you have given something else away. Furthermore, you do not receive a gift from the person to whom you give one. Your gift comes from someone else, and that someone else's gift may come from yet another. Ever in motion, the gift continually moves out of sight and beyond the control of the giver.

What gift might Rodriguez have circulated in exchange for his schooling? A firm believer in the rule of the educated few, Socrates would presumably have had Rodriguez live among and govern the people he labeled "Mexicans without Mexico"[29]—the immigrant workers Rodriguez used to see in Sacramento when he was a teenager. In a democratic society, this paternalistic approach is not acceptable, but other gifts suggest themselves. Teaching the immigrant workers is one such gift, lobbying for better schools for their children is another, helping them improve their working and living conditions is a third.

After praising three of her former teachers, Alice Walker said in a 1972 talk at Sarah Lawrence College, "These women were Sarah Lawrence's gift to me. And when I think of them, I understand that each woman is capable of truly bringing another into the world. This we must all do for each other" (39). She also told students, "Your job, when you leave here—as it was the job of educated women before you—is to change the world. Nothing less or easier than that" (37).

There are countless ways to circulate the gift of education most of which Socrates never contemplated. Who knows! Since writing

Hunger of Memory, Rodriguez may have already given to others the gift his schooling gave him. Or perhaps that memoir represents his gift. But questions remain.

Did Rodriguez have a responsibility to circulate his gift of education to the ethnic group from whence he came? Or could he have lobbied for or lectured about better schools for all those less fortunate than he? Should Ildefonso have only helped out illegal languageless Mexican-American immigrants? Or in exchange for the gift of language could he have tried to improve the lot of others as well? Does Rita, a woman who appears to have devoted not a moment's thought to circulating the gift of education, have a special responsibility to members of the working class? If she becomes a mother, could her labor in transforming her infant from a creature of nature into a member of culture count as her way of circulating the gift? Or, for that matter, does Rita's transformation into an educated woman automatically constitute a gift to those who follow in her footsteps?

It is easy to trivialize the idea of education as a gift by saying that any member of a working-class family who becomes an academic, any woman who becomes a chief of her tribe, any Mexican American who earns a Ph.D., any African American who becomes a law professor or a famous writer is ipso facto a role model and that role modeling is a form of gift circulation. But gifts are consciously and freely given, whereas being a role model is not usually a matter of choice.[30] "I do not object to being a role model, even if I had a choice about the matter, which I probably do not," wrote Guinier.[31]

Rita might not object to being a role model either, but to circulate the gift of education that she herself receives she has to do more than simply be an unconscious or unwitting example for others. Saying that she felt special responsibilities as a black woman law professor, Guinier insisted that "genuine" role models "must lift others as they climb" and need to "nurture their roots not just model their roles."[32] Besides, when someone simply takes something you have, you have not given that individual a gift any more than you have given a burglar a gift when you are forced to hand something over at gunpoint.

In addition to being given deliberately and freely, the gift in gift exchange is imbued with a spirit of thankfulness or appreciation. Hyde cited Alcoholics Anonymous as a prime instance of gift giving, on the one hand because its teachings "are free, a literal gift" and on the other because the twelfth and last step that its members take to recovery is "an act of gratitude: recovered alcoholics help other alcoholics when called upon to do so."[33] In Walker's speech to Sarah Lawrence students this spirit of gratitude or appreciation is palpable, as it also is in an essay she wrote about African-American author Zora Neale Hurston: "*We are a people. A people do not throw their geniuses away.* And if they are thrown away, it is our duty *as artists and as witnesses for the future* to collect them again for the sake of our children, and, if necessary, bone by bone" (92, author's italics).[34]

Lest it be thought that everyone who receives the gift of education has a duty to pass it on to others, it is well to keep in mind that education sometimes does more harm than good. In such instances gratitude will normally be an inappropriate response and so will the desire to pass what has been received along to others. It is only when an educational metamorphosis benefits the one who has undergone it that the question of circulating the gift arises.[35] This is not the place to decide if in all such cases gift circulation is the favored course of action. What does warrant attention here is that in addition to paving the way home, circulating the gift of education can help to dispel the fears of betrayal that often make leaving as well as returning home so difficult.

In *Kaffir Boy*, Mark recalled the visits to South Africa of two African Americans—tennis star Arthur Ashe and boxing champion Bob Foster. Whereas Ashe publicly condemned apartheid and met with government officials in an effort to persuade them to abolish it in sports, Foster distanced himself from the problems facing black South Africans and protested that he was there to box, not to engage in politics. Indeed, Foster went so far as to say that South Africa was not such a bad place after all. Ashe, on the other hand, "was considered a gift. . . . He had become the black messiah sent from strange shores to come liberate us" (238).

The charges of betrayal that occur in connection with culture crossings and the attendant feelings of guilt in our case narratives derive at least part of their force from the assumption that the accused are walking away for good from those they are leaving behind. Yet this is something that cannot be known in advance of the fact. Detractors called Mark a traitor without waiting to see whether he would turn into a Foster or an Ashe: a person who kept the gift of education to himself or who circulated it to others in one form or another. It is by now a matter of record that although Mark left South Africa, he did not walk away from black South Africans.[36] Nor did Esmeralda Santiago turn her back on Puerto Ricans as her schoolmates expected or "sell out" as protesters at an exhibit of the Museum of Modern Art accused her of doing when, years later, she held an administrative position there.[37]

Of course, one who circulates the gift of education does not know what will happen next. Would any of the men to whom Ilde-fonso circulated the gift he received from Schaller be inspired to learn sign language? Would one or more of them acquire sufficient understanding of the dominant culture's practices to be able to pass it along to others? "When I give to someone from whom I do not receive (and yet I do receive elsewhere), it is as if the gift goes around a corner before it comes back. I have to give blindly," wrote Hyde. "Each donation," he added, "is an act of social faith" (16).[38]

ACCULTURATION AS GIFT CIRCULATION

Gift exchange can pave the way home and also ease the journey away from home. In helping young people "who may be traveling a path similar to the one that I took,"[39] a social scientist from a working-class background was doing just this. So too was the college humanities teacher who said, "As a teacher of working-class adults, I do not see myself as a dispenser of wisdom, but rather as a leader of an expedition over terrain that is simply more familiar to me than it is to them."[40] Circulation of the gift can also be said to have been what some white people in South Africa did for Mark Mathabane, what some nuns at the local parochial school did for Richard Rodriguez, what the Wallace family in New York did for Minik, and what Frank does for Rita despite his reservations about academia.

This hit or miss approach can, however, be fraught with danger. Each time Mark played tennis with one of his German acquaintances, "Racist remarks were thrown at us. We made sure never to play at the same place twice in a row" (278). When Mark's tennis partner called the restaurant owners who refused to serve the two of them "bigots," the owners threatened to call the police. In addition, in depending on an individual's having the good fortune to attract a "patron," this hit or miss approach is apt to allow only a select few to succeed. The special attention given "the chosen" is likely to engender resentment in those who are left behind: the preferential treatment will seem unfair and the stay-at-homes will be left wondering if the reason why they have not been favored is that they are not smart enough, talented enough, beautiful enough, or courageous enough. The chosen few in their turn run the risk of becoming "tokens" for a host culture that congratulates itself on including a few outsiders while continuing to be inhospitable to most.

Is there a viable alternative to haphazard gift giving that will smooth the way for individuals who move into new habitats? Cultures of arrival both large and small can acknowledge the existence of educational metamorphoses, recognize that this is a world in which they flourish, and choose to be culture crossing facilitators and easers rather than hinderers and obstructers. To this end they can reject assimilationism.

Although the fitting of culture crossers into a preestablished way of life is what assimilation is all about, it is not the only form that fitting into a cultural entity can take. Consider another equation constructed by students of immigration, namely A + B = C, where the letter C stands for something brand new.[41] This formula makes it clear that in what will here be called "acculturation," the host culture is supposed to change so as to accommodate the crossers even as culture crossers are expected to change to fit into a host culture.[42] In effect, A + B = C rejects the assimilationist premise that the host culture and its portfolio of stock are sacrosanct. It correctly assumes that a school, a university, a military organization, a social class, a profession, an ethnic group, a religion, or any other cultural entity can change; that there is no law, human or otherwise, saying that it must continue to define itself in the way it always has.

A culture that adopts a policy of acculturation will try to ensure that most of its educational agents strive to create an ethos in which newcomers feel welcome rather than like intruders.[43] What this means for a given cultural entity is so tied to context that no detailed programs can be spelled out in advance. At a minimum, however, it involves establishing a welcoming ethos: one in which, for instance, young schoolchildren do not call Asian immigrants "chink eyes," male laws students do not call the women in their classes "feminazi dykes," law schools think twice about the portraits they hang on their walls, the media reconsider its portrayals of women and minorities, and employers avoid discriminatory practices.

Acculturation also allows for the fact that there are different ways to perform the tasks, roles, duties, and practices that comprise a culture's designs for living, and that some of these may be far more congenial to culture crossers than the ones that are presently deemed essential. In the name of assimilation immigrants are expected to rid themselves of the cultural stock that they bring with them so that they can perform their new culture's activities in the "correct" way. The possibility that the stock already in a culture crosser's possession might actually enable him or her to carry out the tasks at hand in an alternative manner is not entertained.

Here Guinier's objections to the term "role model" are relevant. Saying that it "obscures both the struggle and the discrimination involved in opening for other group members real opportunities, not just perceived possibilities" and that "genuine" role models have responsibilities as well as privileges, she suggested that women of color law professors "can be templates for how the role itself might be performed differently." In addition, she said that the presence of women of color on a faculty "might alter the institution's character, introducing a different prism and perspective."[44]

In a similar vein, one working-class woman turned academic remarked, "We can, however, use our 'outsider within' status to challenge the institutions of which we are a part as well as to transform conventional ways of knowing within our respective disciplines."[45] Another stated that when her own performance differs from that of an upper-class white male, as it so often does, she challenges the norms of her society "since how a person performs a role influences the role itself, either by reinforcing others' (and one's own) expectations for the role or by opening up a possibility for change in them."[46]

If women of color law professors or any other culture crossers are to be models or prototypes for how a cultural role might be performed differently, that culture has to reject the assimilationist assumption that "our way of doing things is the only right way." In its place it must substitute the acculturationist proposition that people who differ from the norms of the group can actually enrich it.

Acculturation can be considered a special case of circulating the gift of education. When gift exchange paves the way home, the gift that is being circulated was previously given the returnee by the culture of arrival and is now being passed along to the culture of departure. When a culture of arrival embraces acculturation the situation is reversed. The culture crosser is again the gift giver, but in this instance the gift of education that was earlier received by the newcomer from the culture of departure is now being circulated in the culture of arrival.

The policy represented by A + B = C requires not only that a culture of arrival be welcoming to culture crossers, although this itself may not be an easy task. It demands that the culture accept the gifts that these immigrants bring with them and proceed to circulate them. As it happens, it is in the interest of cultures of arrival to do so, for they are likely to profit immensely from incorporating in their portfolios some of the stock that newcomers possess. The authors of a late–twentieth-century study of Latino adolescents pointed out that immigrants "bring a special energy (perhaps to compensate for all the losses that are inherent in immigration) that is positive, when well harnessed."[47] This may be the least of the benefits to be derived from welcoming the gifts of culture crossers. In 2005, even as an umpire halted a teenage baseball game in Massachusetts because a coach cried out to his pitcher in Spanish,[48] the general manager of the New York Mets was making news by signing up players from the Dominican Republic. "Omar Minaya is reinventing the Mets by embracing the Latinization of professional baseball," read one headline.[49]

In the 1920s German sociologist Karl Mannheim wrote that if there were no new generations, there would be no changed relationship of individuals to a culture's stock; and without this latter there would be no cultural renewal.[50] Mannheim's point that new generations contribute to cultural innovation is well taken, especially when his talk of "new generations" is interpreted broadly. For newborns are not a culture's only source of new blood. Culture crossers can also be a wellspring of cultural renewal. In fact, they can serve this function for their cultures of departure as well as their cultures of arrival.

CIRCULATING THE GIFT IN TWO DIRECTIONS

Understandably, discussions about immigration have tended to take it for granted that the host culture—the "A" in our equations—is the culture of arrival.[51] Thus, the tacit assumption has been that $A + B = A$ and $A + B = C$ are forward-looking processes. Yet according to our case studies, the pain experienced by those who undergo educational metamorphosis is as apt to spring from the culture of departure as from the culture of arrival. Acculturation and assimilation are best interpreted, therefore, as both forward and backward looking policies. Even as an individual wants to fit into the culture of arrival without being a freak, he or she hopes to be able to go back home to the culture of departure without being a misfit. And just as cultures of arrival can make entry very difficult for newcomers, cultures of departure can be unfriendly both to those who seek to make culture crossings and to those who, having made one or more, wish to go back home.

To be sure, some cultures of departure may actively help those who wish to travel and eagerly welcome back those who return home. Others, however, are as scornful of the gifts their returnees bear as cultures of arrival are contemptuous of the gifts brought to them by newcomers. "I used to wonder how I escaped the anti-intellectualism of the working class," wrote one academic."[52] "My parents wouldn't talk to me. . . . It embarrassed them to tell people their son had gone to college and was now studying religion and teaching high school," wrote another.[53]

The problems returnees face are understandable. When one considers that ways of walking, talking, eating, drinking, and dressing are apt to be deeply entrenched elements of a culture's design for living, it is scarcely surprising that even the seemingly insignificant changes that occur in the course of an educational metamorphosis have the potential to rupture relationships. Furthermore, educational metamorphoses do not only affect an individual's ways of walking, talking, eating, drinking, and dressing. They transform attitudes and values. Think of the Rita/Denny dispute. If Denny is going to ease rather than hinder Rita's return home—if, indeed, he is going to facilitate her crossing into academia in the first place—he will have to stop burning her books and start viewing "higher" education in a positive light. The other members of her culture of departure will have to make this by no means insignificant change of attitude as well.

Yet why should Denny and his friends be expected to change their opinions of the culture Rita is entering if, as research on higher education indicates, the academy looks down on them? And why suppose that Rita would want to go home again if in the course of her studies she learned to disparage blue-collar work and to distance herself from her working-class background and her everyday experience?[54] To generalize, is it really plausible to expect cultural wholes and their countless parts—of which academia is but one example—to purge themselves of the racism, sexism, classism, xenophobia, and the rest that lurk behind the hostility to people who appear different? And even if this were likely to happen, are not full-fledged members of both cultures of arrival and cultures of departure apt to persist in the belief that the price of entry and return is conformity to its existing mores?[55]

It is a utopian dream to assume that most cultural entities would give up long-standing attitudes, values, and practices without a struggle. Still, who knows how much relief might be produced if cultural entities of all sizes and shapes were to keep in mind that even their most long-standing members were once newcomers and to reflect upon their own attitudes and behavior toward those who embark on culture crossings, those who enter new groups, and those who want to go back home again. Who knows how many remedies would be found if cultures were to make it a general practice to circulate the gift of education to those who seek to enter them, those who want to return to them, and those who wish to embark on new journeys.

The question remains whether a policy that eases the way for culture crossers will prevent them from being outsiders who give what is arguably the most important gift of all. In *Three Guineas*, a 1938 essay on women, education, and war, Virginia Woolf wrote that women can best help men prevent war "not by repeating your words and following your methods but by finding new words and creating new methods. We can best help you to prevent war not by joining your society but by remaining outside your society but in cooperation with its aim."[56] In 2002 Lani Guinier and Gerald Torres struck a similar note when they wrote, "The reality is that agitation by people of color has made this a freer and, in a strict sense, more liberal culture."[57] Adding that "racial group identification can turn a psychology of perceived individual weakness into a politics of collective strength,"[58] they concluded, "Racialized communities can represent sites for democratic renewal."[59]

It is true that insiders are often unable or unwilling to perceive the problems inherent in the cultures to which they belong, let alone criticize them, and it is also the case that outsider critiques can be transformative. Yet it is equally true that too much suffering can preclude the kind of constructive cultural critique and renewal for which outsiders are renowned. Indeed, culture crossers whose pains are unalleviated can become destructive forces in their cultures of arrival.

Fortunately there is no need to choose between two untenable alternatives: a culture's blunting the critical perceptions of culture crossers by easing the way for culture crossers or else receiving the gifts of cultural critique and renewal from culture crossers while doing nothing about their suffering. In the first place, the outsider/insider distinction is a matter of degree, not a sharp dichotomy. Thus, a person whose way is eased may feel more of an insider than under a policy of assimilation, yet not so much of an insider as to lose his or her critical perspective. Besides, if Woolf is correct that those in a position to give the gifts of constructive cultural critique and renewal must share the culture's basic aims—and she would seem to be—then some degree of insider status is surely required.

Second, there is no reason to believe that if the policy of acculturation were understood as a special case of gift circulation, all the suffering to which educational metamorphoses give rise would be eradicated and all culture crossers would become full-fledged insiders. On the contrary, just as assimilation affects different individuals differently, so would this more inclusive approach. But then, to the extent that alienation, loss, and fears of betrayal really are the sources of constructive outsider critiques, these last would not be forfeited.

Just as Minik must at first have felt overwhelmed by the sight of New York harbor, one can easily be overwhelmed by the thought of the cultural changes that are required if the way is to be eased for culture crossers. How tempting it is when confronted with such blooming, buzzing confusion to adopt the line of least resistance and act as if educational metamorphoses do not occur or else are of no importance! In this world of ours it is, however, unrealistic to ignore their existence. And given that educational metamorphoses are not personal transformations or identity changes pure and simple but composite phenomena that give rise to the pain of loss, the fear of betrayal, and an abiding sense of alienation and marginality, it is foolhardy to deny their importance.

If there were no possible relief for those who undergo educational metamorphoses, there might be no good reason to call attention on the problem. If their travails made no difference to the cultures involved, there might be no need to turn the spotlight on it. But the pains can be alleviated, if not eradicated, and the gifts that these culture crossers have it in their power to circulate to their cultures of arrival and departure are potentially a wellspring of cultural renewal.

In light of our case studies it need hardly be added that when the subject is educational metamorphoses it is essential to think beyond the confines of school. School can contribute to the solution of the problems to which these personal transformations/culture crossings give rise, but just as school is not the only educational agent that brings about these radical changes in people—or even, perhaps, the most important agent—it cannot single-handedly remedy the problems they cause.

As in the adage that it takes a village to raise a child, it will take the major portion of a culture's educational agents—governmental bureaus, religious organizations, the print and electronic media, businesses, advertising agencies, families, community associations, and so on and so forth—to make circulation of the gift of education a cultural norm. It cannot be otherwise, for large-scale cultural change is necessarily a culture-wide project.

NOTES

1. Janet McDonald, *Project Girl* (New York: Farrar, Strauss, and Giroux, 1999), 30.

2. Saundra Gardner, "What's a Nice Working-Class Girl Like You Doing in a Place Like This?" in *Working-Class Women in the Academy*, ed. Michelle M. Tokarczyk and Elizabeth A. Fay (Amherst: University of Massachusetts Press, 1993), 49.

3. Gardner, "What's a Nice Working-Class Girl Like You Doing in a Place Like This?," 50.

4. Donna Langston, "Who Am I Now? The Politics of Class Identity," in Tokarczyk and Fay, *Working-Class Women*, 67.

5. Valerie Miner, "Writing and Teaching with Class," in Tokarczyk and Fay, *Working-Class Women*, 79.

6. Renny Christopher, "A Carpenter's Daughter," in *This Fine Place So Far from Home*, ed. C. L. Barney Dews and Carolyn Leste Law (Philadelphia: Temple University Press, 1995), 150.

7. M. Elaine Mar, *Paper Daughter* (New York: Perennial, 1999), 292.

8. Michael Schwalbe, "The Work of Professing (A Letter to Home)," in Dews and Law, *This Fine Place*, 309.

9. Mary Cappello, "Useful Knowledge," in Dews and Law, *This Fine Place*, 133.

10. Esmeralda Santiago, *Almost a Woman* (New York: Vintage, 1998), 31.

11. Esmeralda Santiago, *The Turkish Lover* (New York: Da Capo Press, 2004), 19.

12. *Adaptation, amalgamation, acculturation,* and *integration* are some of the other terms used to designate the process represented by A + B = A. For a discussion of the difference between assimilation and what will in these pages be called *acculturation* see Ralph Beals, "Acculturation," in *Anthropology Today*, ed. A. L. Kroeber (Chicago: University of Chicago Press, 1953), 621–41.

13. Santiago, *Almost a Woman*, 37.

14. Santiago, *Almost a Woman*, 50.

15. McDonald, *Project Girl*, 66.

16. Lorene Cary, *Black Ice* (New York: Vintage Books, 1991), 4.

17. Cary, *Black Ice*, 6.

18. Donna Langston, "Who Am I Now? The Politics of Class Identity," in Tokarczyk and Fay, *Working-Class Women*, 60.

19. The term *home* is so elastic that it can even be applied to a place where a person has never actually lived. See, e.g., Takeyuki (Gaku) Tsuda, "When Home Is Not the Homeland: The Case of Japanese Brazilian Ethnic Return Migration," in *Homecomings*, ed. Fran Markowitz and Anders H. Stefansson (Lanham, MD: Lexington Books, 2004), 125–45; Lisa Anteby-Yemini, "Promised Land, Imagined Homelands: Ethiopian Jews' Immigration to Israel," in Markowitz and Stefansson, *Homecomings* 147–64.

20. Irvin Peckham, "Complicity in Class Codes: The Exclusionary Function of Education," in Dews and Law, *This Fine Place*, 274.

21. Rosa Maria Pegueros, "*Todos Vuyelven*: From Potrero Hill to UCLA," in Dews and Law, *This Fine Place*, 105.

22. Pam Annas, "Pass the Cake: The Politics of Gender, Class, and Text in the Academic Workplace," in Tokarczyk and Fay, *Working-Class Women*, 169.

23. C. L. Barney Dews, "Afterword" in Dews and Law, *This Fine Place,* 335.

24. Peckham, "Complicity in Class Codes," 274.

25. Transcript, *Daughter from Danang, American Experience,* Public Broadcasting System. Page references are in parentheses in the text.

26. Cf. Anders H. Stefansson, "Sarajevo Suffering: Homecoming and the Hierarchy of Homeland Hardship," in Markowitz and Stefansson, *Homecomings,* 54–75; Bayo Holsey, "Transatlantic Dreaming: Slavery, Tourism, and Diasporic Encounters," in Markowitz and Stefansson, *Homecomings,* 166–82.

27. Plato, *Republic,* trans. G. M. A. Grube (Indianapolis, IN: Hackett Publishing, 1974), 518d.

28. Lewis Hyde, *The Gift* (New York: Vintage, 1979), 4. For an interesting discussion of Hyde's account of the practice of gift giving, see Dianne Margolis, *The Fabric of Self* (New Haven, CT: Yale University Press, 1998).

29. Richard Rodriguez, *Days of Obligation* (New York: Penguin Books, 1992), 52.

30. Which is not to say that in particular circumstances a person may not feel duty bound to give a gift.

31. Lani Guinier, "Models and Mentors," in Lani Guinier, Michelle Fine, and Jane Balin, *Becoming Gentlemen* (Boston: Beacon Press, 1997), 90.

32. Guinier, "Models and Mentors," 94.

33. Hyde, *The Gift,* 46.

34. Some may object that the element of appreciation or gratitude in the idea of gift circulation makes this a paternalistic practice. There is no assumption of a hierarchical relationship between gift giver and recipient in gift exchange, however. Granted, the two parties to the exchange are not identical: At the very least, when the exchange begins only one party to it has the gift. Nevertheless, just as in ordinary gift giving the two parties can be social, political, and economic equals, so they can be in gift exchanges.

35. Those who hold that education is a human right may in their turn protest that the very idea of education as gift conflicts with this conception. But even if something is a right, the practice can still be received as a gift. Consider the first amendment to the U.S. Constitution. It leaves no doubt that in the United States freedom of religion is a right. Nonetheless, it is perfectly legitimate to view freedom to worship as one pleases as a gift that the framers of the Constitution gave to future generations of U.S. citizens.

36. In a sequel to *Kaffir Boy,* Mark wrote: "In my lectures across the country I have urged students and other Americans eager to help to organize book and clothing drives and send the items to Alexandra and

other ghettos. . . . I am also working on raising money for the construction of a library in Alexandra. . . . One of my greatest joys has been in sharing with young Americans my life story and convictions, and acting as a role model. . . . I know that somewhere there is a young black or white child to whom my life story will act as an inspiration. I know this because the life stories of Arthur Ashe and Richard Wright acted as inspirations to me. . . . I also take pride in helping young black South Africans come over to America to study." Mark Mathabane, *Kaffir Boy in America* (New York: Collier Books, 1989), 291–93.

37. Santiago, *The Turkish Lover*, 135.

38. Hyde, *The Gift*, 16.

39. George Martin, "In the Shadow of My Old Kentucky Home," in Dews and Law, *This Fine Place*, 86.

40. Rose Zimbardo, "Teaching the Working Woman," in Tokarczyk and Fay, *Working-Class Women*, 208.

41. It should be noted that the process represented by the equation A + B = C is very different from the one represented by the equation A + B = A + B. In this latter process—sometimes called *multiculturalism*—a new individual or group joins an existing group but neither one changes.

42. Here again confusion reigns. The process represented by A + B = C that is being called here *acculturation* is sometimes referred to as *adaptation*, sometimes as *amalgamation*, and sometimes as *integration*.

43. This is not to say that every single cultural group and institution within a given cultural whole must try to ease the way for culture crossers. Something can be a policy or a priority of a cultural whole without being a policy or a priority of each of its parts. If, for example, the United States were to become a culture in which circulation of the gift of education was standard practice, it would not be necessary for a closed group like the Amish to throw open its doors to outsiders. All that would be required is that most dominant cultural groups within the United States welcome culture crossers rather than rebuff them. Nor does the idea of facilitating culture crossings entail that anything goes. To urge that cultures should ease the way for the many kinds of immigrants in their midst is not to say that someone with no medical training should be allowed to perform brain surgery or that a symphony orchestra should hire someone for its string section who cannot play a musical instrument.

44. Guinier, "Models and Mentors," 90.

45. Saundra Gardner, "What's a Nice Working-Class Girl Like You Doing in a Place Like This?" in Tokarczyk and Fay, *Working-Class Women*, 56. For an interesting discussion of the outside-insider distinction see, e.g., David A. Crocker, "Cross-Cultural Criticism and Development Ethics, *Philosophy & Public Policy Quarterly*, vol. 24 (Summer), 2004, 2–7.

46. Sharon Odair, "Vestments and Vested Interests: Academia, the Working Class, and Affirmative Action," in Tokarczyk and Fay, *Working-Class Women*, 204.

47. Carola and Marcelo Suárez-Orozco, *Trans-formations* (Palo Alto, CA: Stanford University Press, 1995), 189–90.

48. Christina M. Silva and Raja Mishra, "Umpire's Call Gets Unheard-of Result," *Boston Globe*, July 30, 2005, B1.

49. Jonathan Mahler, "Building the *Béisbol* Brand," *New York Times Magazine*, July 31, 2005, 22.

50. Karl Mannheim, "The Problem of Generations," in *Essays on the Sociology of Knowledge*, ed. P. Kecskemeti (London: Routledge and Kegan Paul, 1952), 276–320.

51. For a notable exception see Markowitz and Stefansson, *Homecomings*. Studies of immigration in this volume support the conclusion that just as it is difficult to fit into cultures of arrival it is difficult to fit back into cultures of departure.

52. Naton Leslie, "You Were Raised Better Than That," in Dews and Law, *This Fine Place*, 69.

53. Stephen Garger, "Bronx Syndrome," in Dews and Law, *This Fine Place*, 46.

54. See, e.g., Jake Ryan and Charles Sackrey, *Strangers in Paradise* (Boston: South End Press, 1984); cf. Jane Roland Martin, *Coming of Age in Academe* (New York: Routledge, 2000).

55. Indeed, even in the case of broad-based social movements that seek to bring newcomers into the dominant culture, the assimilationist tendency is apt to be strong. Thus, for example, while some members of the movement that transformed Sandra Bartky into a feminist insisted that for women to be full-fledged equal members the host culture would have to undergo radical change, others held that so long as women acquired the same skills, knowledge, attitudes, and values of men they would be treated equally and there would be no need to transform U.S. society. The same kind of split characterized the Civil Rights Movement that transformed Alice Walker, with some members insisting that a transformation of the white man's culture is required and others holding that assimilation into the mainstream will bring racial equality.

56. Virginia Woolf, *Three Guineas* (New York: Harcourt, Brace, Jovanovich, 1938), 143.

57. Lani Guinier and Gerald Torres, *The Miner's Canary* (Cambridge, MA: Harvard University Press, 2002), 52.

58. Guinier and Torres, *Miner's Canary*, 86.

59. Guinier and Torres, *Miner's Canary*, 100. It should be added that there is no need for a policy aiming at facilitating culture crossings to erase race, gender, class, or any other politically or socially significant category.

Conclusion

One late October afternoon in 2005 I knocked on an office door at the University of Massachusetts in Boston. I had earlier telephoned the occupant to say that I did not want to finish the book I was writing about educational metamorphoses without first speaking to him. Having begun this volume with an account of a student who left the university rather than desert his friends and family, I thought it only fitting to finish with the story of someone who stayed the course. And so there I was, tape recorder in hand, about to interview the highly regarded scholar and distinguished professor of liberal arts and education, Donaldo Macedo, who had been my student in the early 1970s.

From that interview I extract here only the bare bones of an educational metamorphosis in which an immigrant for whom English was not a first or even a second language[1] was transformed into an American academic. Upon arriving as a teenager in Boston from Cape Verde with his parents and his six brothers and sisters, Donaldo went first to a day school where he was taught English and then to Boston English High. In high school the challenge for him was not the subject matter of his math, science, history, and English courses but the English language itself. Sadly, just as eighteenth-century scholars equated Victor's intellectual ability with his capacity to learn a first language, Donaldo's guidance counselor equated his intelligence with his capacity to learn a third. After taking the exam that U.S. colleges tend to rely on when admitting students and feeling "utterly defeated" by the verbal portion of it, Donaldo went to see this man. In what amounts to a replay of Malcolm X's encounter in junior high, the counselor told his advisee to forget about college. Said Donaldo, "He began this long dissertation about how Americans had this 30,000 word vocabulary and I never would, so I should go to Franklin Institute and become a TV repairman."

Donaldo had not come to the United States to repair television sets, however. "It's not that I looked down on the position. I was working as a mechanic and my Dad was too. . . . But my parents wanted to move so we would be educated. I was the first of seven siblings so I had this major responsibility. If I would fail I would not set the example and be a role model for my brothers and sisters." At this critical juncture a "patron" in the form of another guidance counselor at the school saw him in the hall looking upset and asked what the trouble was.[2] "He told me to bring in my records from Cape Verde. 'You are going to college, you are going to college, you are going to college.' He said it three times. On my way home I picked up an application to U Mass Boston and I got accepted with my 280 SAT score in English."

The University of Massachusetts, Boston, of the 1970s can aptly be described as an educational agent committed to circulating the gift of higher education to poor people in the Boston area, to minorities, and to immigrants. This is not to say that it carried out its mission as well as it might have. "No one was around to advise people like myself. . . . So you had to navigate the labyrinth by yourself," said Donaldo. Before he learned to do so effectively, he enrolled in an English course only to have the professor tell him, "Sonny, I think you should learn English and then take my course." Nevertheless, the student body was sufficiently diverse that he was able to find a support group of African American and Latino students. "We used to tell each other, 'Take so-and-so.' 'I've got a great teacher.' That's how we survived. . . . I became an investigator of professors with sensitivity."

When I asked Donaldo what had happened to the other members of that informal network, he told me that some had become teachers but many had dropped out of school. "I am an accident of history," he said. "I had tremendous family support. I was fortunate enough to meet great teachers. If I hadn't I might also have dropped out." Our historical accident graduated from college, thus becoming the role model for his siblings that his parents expected him to be and that he himself wanted to be. With the urging of one of his professors he then went on to graduate school where he "fell in love" with the field of linguistics. If, as Guinier said, some people "take no account of how they arrived at their destination" (90), Donaldo is one who did not forget. Returning to his alma mater as a faculty member, this Cape Verdean immigrant to the United States with a 280 verbal SAT score became a professor with sensitivity to new generations of students like himself and a scholar whose research and writing focus on issues of education in general and language learning in particular.

When in the course of writing this book I discussed my case studies with others, someone invariably expressed concern that in developing the idea of educational metamorphoses I have made talk about the aims of education pointless. The assumption seems to be that if education is as unruly and unpredictable as my materials suggest, then it is useless to set goals for children to meet since the objectives will not be achieved. But to draw attention to the great changes that education brings about in people is not to invalidate the attempts of parents, teachers, politicians, and philosophers throughout the ages to specify what should be taught and learned. It is, rather, to remind one and all that education is far more than a purveyor of knowledge and skills, attitudes, and values: It is a maker and shaper of every single member of human culture.

Thus, the moral to be drawn from our case studies of educational metamorphoses is not that goals cannot be set, but that there are many more aims to choose from than are listed in most philosophies. There is, for example, the aim suggested by Donaldo's case that educators of every stripe be sensitive to the situation of immigrants in both the narrow and the broad sense of the term. There is also the aim suggested by Victor's case that no child be left behind on the crossing into human culture, and the one suggested by Malcolm X's case that educational metamorphoses which do the individual more harm than good should be prevented. In addition there is the aim that education's agents both large and small facilitate the culture crossings of what are deemed to be benign or beneficial educational metamorphoses. And there is the overarching aim that those who receive the gift of education become in their turn its circulators.

A second and perhaps even more important moral to be drawn from my interview with Donaldo and our other case studies is that there is far more at issue where education is concerned than reading levels; far more than mathematical, historical, scientific, or computer literacy; indeed, far more than all these issues combined. At stake is the kind of people we want ourselves, our friends and relations, our neighbors, and the other members of our culture to be; and also the kind of people we want the children, grandchildren, and great grandchildren of all of the above to be.

Throughout this book questions about educational metamorphoses have arisen that cry out for systematic research. To cite but a few: How often does the average person undergo an educational metamorphosis? Do some individuals undergo many more metamorphoses than others? In what contexts are educational metamorphoses likely to occur? Are some cultures easier to leave than others? Are some cultures easier to cross into? New theoretical frameworks that include educational metamorphoses in their mappings of the educational terrain are also needed. But research and theory, no matter how illuminating, are not enough.

Academic enterprises cannot take the place of public discussion about education as one of the fundamental makers and shapers of our children and ourselves. Research and theory cannot supplant culturewide reflection about how to promote beneficial educational metamorphoses and thwart the development of harmful ones. And although they can jog our memories, they are no substitutes for what is especially needed, namely a kind of mass remembrance and review of our own firsthand experience. Once we apprehend that we are all case studies of educational metamorphoses, great numbers of us will find it imperative to circulate the gift of education to those who are following in our footsteps. If in addition we acknowledge that there may yet be more personal transformations/culture crossings in our own futures, who knows how many of us will be inspired to ease the way for those who are already setting out on brand new journeys.

NOTES

1. Cape Verde Creole was his first language and Portuguese his second.
2. The patron was John O'Bryant, who later became the first African-American school committee member in Boston.

Bibliography

Alcott, Louisa May. 1936. *Little Women*. Boston: Little Brown.

Allen, Jeffner. 1984. "Motherhood: The Annihilation of Women," in Joyce Trebilcot, ed., *Mothering*. Totowa, NJ: Rowman and Allenheld, 314–30.

Annas, Pam. 1993. "Pass the Cake: The Politics of Gender, Class, and Text in the Academic Workplace," in Michelle M. Tokarczyk and Elizabeth A. Fay, eds., *Working-Class Women in the Academy*. Amherst: University of Massachusetts Press, 165–78.

Anteby-Yemini, Lisa. 2004. "Promised Land, Imagined Homelands: Ethiopian Jews' Immigration to Israel," in Fran Markowitz and Anders H. Stefansson, eds., *Homecomings*. Lanham, MD: Lexington Books, 147–64.

Arana, Marie. 2001. *American Chica*. New York: Dial Press.

Bailyn, Bernard. 1960. *Education in the Forming of American Society*. New York: Viking.

Bartky, Sandra. 1990. *Femininity and Domination*. New York: Routledge.

Beals, Ralph. 1953. "Acculturation," in A. L. Kroeber, ed., *Anthropology Today*. Chicago: University of Chicago Press.

Bidney, David. 1953. *Theoretical Anthropology*. New York: Columbia University Press.

Black, Laurel Johnson. 1995. "Stupid Rich Bastards," in C. L. Barney Dews, and Carolyn Leste Law, eds., *This Fine Place So Far from Home*. Philadelphia: Temple University Press, 13–25.

Blackmore, Susan. 1999. *The Meme Machine*. Oxford: Oxford University Press.

Bornstein, Kate. 1995. *Gender Outlaw*. New York: Vintage Books.

Boylan, Jennifer Finney. 2003. *She's Not There*. New York: Broadway Books.

Bronte, Charlotte. 1997. *Jane Eyre*. New York: Signet Books.

Brumbaugh, Robert S., and Lawrence, Nathaniel M. 1963. *Philosophers of Education: Six Essays on Western Thought*. Boston: Houghton Mifflin.

Canton, Cecil E. 2002. "From Slaveship to Scholarship: A Narrative of the Political and Social Transformation of an African American Educator," in Lila Jacobs, José Cintrón, and Cecil E. Canton, eds., *The Politics of Survival in Academia*. Lanham, MD: Roman & Littlefield, 15–32.

Cappello, Mary. 1995. "Useful Knowledge," in C. L. Barney Dews, and Carolyn Leste Law, eds., *This Fine Place So Far from Home*. Philadelphia: Temple University Press, 127–36.

Cary, Lorene. 1991. *Black Ice*. New York: Vintage Books.

Christopher, Renny. 1995. "A Carpenter's Daughter," in C. L. Barney Dews, and Carolyn Leste Law, eds., *This Fine Place So Far from Home*. Philadelphia: Temple University Press, 137–50.

Clifford, James. 1997. *Routes*. Cambridge, MA: Harvard University Press.

Cohen, Rosetta Marantz. 1998. "Class Consciousness and Its Consequences: The Impact of an Elite Education on Mature, Working-Class Women." *American Educational Research Journal*, vol. 356, no. 3, 353–75.

Cremin, Lawrence. 1965. *The Genius of American Education*. New York: Vintage.

Crocker, David A. 2004. "Cross-Cultural Criticism and Development Ethics." *Philosophy & Public Policy Quarterly*, vol. 24 (Summer), 2–7.

de Beauvoir, Simone. 1961. *The Second Sex*. New York: Bantam Books.

Dewey, John. 1961. *Democracy and Education*. New York: Macmillan.

———. 1963 (1938). *Experience and Education*. New York: Macmillan.

———. 1976. "The Influence of Darwinism on Philosophy," in James Gouinlock, ed., *The Moral Writings of John Dewey*. New York: Hafner Press, 24–55.

Dews, C. L. Barney. 1993. Afterword. In C. L. Barney Dews, and Carolyn Leste Law, eds. *This Fine Place So Far from Home*. Philadelphia: Temple University Press, 332–36.

Dews, C. L. Barney, and Law, Carolyn Leste, eds. 1993. *This Fine Place So Far from Home*. Philadelphia: Temple University Press.

Diamond, Jared. 1999. *Guns, Germs, and Steel*. New York: Norton.

Dickens, Charles. n.d. *David Copperfield*. New York: Walter J. Black.

Diller, Ann. 2004. "The Search for Wise Love in Education: What Can We Learn from the Brahmaviharas?" in Daniel Liston, and Jim Garrison, eds., *Teaching, Learning, and Loving*. New York: Routledge Falmer.

Drabble, Margaret. 1965. *Thank You All Very Much (The Millstone)*. New York: New American Library.

———. 1972. *The Needle's Eye*. New York: Alfred A. Knopf.

———. 1982. "With All My Love, (Signed) Mama," in Susan Cahill, ed., *Motherhood*. New York: Avon

Dubois, W. E. B. 1965. "The Souls of Black Folk," in *Three Negro Classics*. New York: Avon Books.

Eliot, George. 1986. *Daniel Deronda*. London: Penguin.

English, Bella. 2004. "Life after Lulu." *Boston Globe*, November 10, D1, 4–5.

Firestone, Shulamith. 1971. *The Dialectic of Sex*. New York: Bantam Books.

Fishel, Elizabeth. 2000. *Reunion*. New York: Random House.

Foucault, Michel. 1980. *Power/Knowledge: Selected Interviews and Other Writings 1972–1977*. New York: Pantheon.

Fullinwider, Robert K. 2003. "Multicultural Education," in Randall Curren, ed., *A Companion to the Philosophy of Education*. Malden, MA: Blackwell Publishing, chap. 34.

Gardner, Saundra. 1993. "What's a Nice Working-Class Girl Like You Doing in a Place Like This?" in Michelle M. Tokarczyk, and Elizabeth A. Fay, eds., *Working-Class Women in the Academy*. Amherst: University of Massachusetts Press, 49–59.

Garger, Stephen. 1993. "Bronx Syndrome," in C. L. Barney Dews and Carolyn Leste, eds., *This Fine Place So Far from Home*. Philadelphia: Temple University Press, 41–53.

Geertz, Clifford. 1973. *The Interpretation of Cultures*. New York: Basic Books.

Gleick, James. 1987. *Chaos*. New York: Penguin Books.

Goodlad, John I., Mantel-Bromley, Corinne, and Goodlad, Stephen John. 2004. *Education for Everyone*. San Francisco: Jossey-Bass.

Gray, J. Glenn. 1970. *The Warriors*. New York: Harper and Row.

Guinier, Lani, and Torres, Gerald. 2002. *The Miner's Canary*. Cambridge, MA: Harvard University Press.

Guinier, Lani. 1997. "Models and Mentors," in Lani Guinier, Michelle Fine, and Jane Balin, *Becoming Gentlemen*. Boston: Beacon Press, 85–97.

Guinier, Lani, Fine, Michelle, and Balin, Jane. 1997. *Becoming Gentlemen*. Boston: Beacon Press.

Hacking, Ian. 1986. "The Archeology of Foucault," in D. C. Hoy, ed., *Foucault: A Critical Reader*. Oxford: Blackwell.

Hamilton, Edith. 1953. *Mythology*. New York: New American Library.

Handlin, Oscar. 1951. *The Uprooted*. Boston: Little, Brown.

Hansen, Marcus Lee. 1996 (1938). "The Problem of the Third Generation Immigrant," in Werner Sollors, ed., *Theories of Ethnicity*. New York: Washington Square Press, 202–15.

Harper, Kenn. 2000. *Give Me My Father's Body*. New York: Washington Square Press.

Harringon, Mona. 1995. *Women Lawyers*. New York: Plume Books.

Hoijer, Harry. 1953. "The Relation of Language to Culture," in A. L. Kroeber, ed., *Anthropology Today*. Chicago: University of Chicago Press, 554–73.

Holsey, Bayo. 2004. "Transatlantic Dreaming: Slavery, Tourism, and Diasporic Encounters," in Fran Markowitz and Anders H. Stefansson, eds., *Homecomings*, 166–82.

Horowitz, Helen. 1984. *Alma Mater*. Boston: Beacon Press.

Houppert, Karen. 2005. "Military Recruiters Are Now Targeting Sixth Graders. Who's Next?" *The Nation*, September 12, 15–20.

Hyde, Lewis. 1983. *The Gift*. New York: Vintage Books.

Hynes, Samuel. 2003. *The Growing Season*. New York: Viking.

Illich, Ivan. 1972. *Deschooling Society*. New York: Harrow.

James, William. 1987 (1910). "The Moral Equivalent of War," in Howard P. Kainz, ed., *Philosophical Perspectives on Peace*. Athens: Ohio University Press, 213–25.

———. 1950 (1890). *The Principles of Psychology*, vol. 1. New York: Dover Publications.

———. 1961. *Varieties of Religious Experience*. New York: Collier Books.

Kafka, Franz. 1992. "The Metamorphosis," in *The Metamorphosis and Other Stories*. New York: Penguin Books, 64–110.

Kagan, Jerome, and Nancy Snidman. 2004. *The Long Shadow of Temperament*. Cambridge, MA: Harvard University Press.

Kuhn, Thomas S. 1970. *The Structure of Scientific Revolutions*. Chicago: University of Chicago Press, 2nd ed.

Kumiko, Ikuta. 2000. "What Are the Implications of the Teaching and Learning Method of Traditional Japanese Artistic Performances." *Bildung und Erziehung*, vol. 53, no. 5 (December 2000), 429–39.

Lane, Harlan. 1976. *The Wild Boy of Aveyron*. Cambridge, MA: Harvard University Press.

Lang, Dwight. 1995. "The Social Construction of a Working-Class Academic," in C. L. Barney Dews, and Carolyn Leste Law, eds., *This Fine Place So Far from Home*. Philadelphia: Temple University Press, 159–76.

Langston, Donna. 1993. "Who Am I Now? The Politics of Class Identity," in Michelle M. Tokarczyk, and Elizabeth A. Fay, eds., *Working-Class Women in the Academy*. Amherst: University of Massachusetts Press, 60–72.

Lapaglia, Nancy. 1995. "Working-Class Woman as Academics: Seeing in Two Directions, Awkwardly," in C. L. Barney Dews, and Carolyn Leste Law, eds., *This Fine Place So Far from Home*. Philadelphia: Temple University Press, 177–86.

Law, Carolyn Leste. 1993. "Introduction" in C. L. Barney Dews, and Carolyn Leste Law, eds., *This Fine Place So Far from Home*. Philadelphia: Temple University Press, 1–10.

Leslie, Naton. 1993. "You Were Raised Better Than That," in C. L. Barney Dews and Carolyn Leste Law, eds., *This Fine Place So Far from Home.* Philadelphia: Temple University Press, 66–74.

Lipsky, David. 2003. *Absolutely American.* Boston: Houghton Mifflin.

Llewellyn, Richard. 1997. *How Green Was My Valley.* New York: Simon and Schuster.

Lumpkin, John J. 2005. "Marine General Says It's 'Fun' to Shoot Some in Combat," *Boston Globe*, February 2, 2005, A4.

Mannheim, Karl. 1952. "The Problem of Generations," in P. Kecskjemeti, ed. *Essays in the Sociology of Knowledge.* London: Routledge & Kegal Paul.

Mankiller, Wilma. 1993. *Mankiller.* New York: St. Martin's Press.

Mar, M. Elaine. 1999. *Paper Daughter.* New York: Perennial.

Margolis, Dianne. 1998. *The Fabric of Self.* New Haven, CT: Yale University Press.

Markowitz, Fran, and Stefansson, Anders H., eds. 2004. *Homecomings.* Lanham, MD: Lexington Books.

Martin, George. 1995. "In the Shadow of My Old Kentucky Home," in C. L. Barney Dews, and Carolyn Leste Law, eds., *This Fine Place So Far from Home.* Philadelphia: Temple University Press, 75–86.

Martin, Jane Roland. 1985. *Reclaiming a Conversation.* New Haven, CT: Yale University Press.

——. 1994a. *Changing the Educational Landscape.* New York: Routledge.

——. 1994b. "Methodological Essentialism, False Difference, and Other Dangerous Traps," *Signs*, vol. 19, 630–57.

——. 2000. *Coming of Age in Academe.* New York: Routledge.

——. 2002. *Cultural Miseducation.* New York: Teachers College Press.

——. 2004. "The Love Gap in the Philosophy of Education Text," in Daniel Liston, and Jim Garrison, eds., *Teaching, Learning, and Loving.* New York: Routledge Falmer, 21–34.

Mathabane, Mark. 1989. *Kaffir Boy in America.* New York: Collier Books.

——. 1986. *Kaffir Boy.* New York: Simon and Schuster.

Maushart, Susan. 2000. *The Mask of Motherhood.* New York: Penguin Books.

Mayes, Frances. 1997. *Under the Tuscan Sun.* New York: Broadway Books.

McDonald, Janet. 1999. *Project Girl.* New York: Farrar, Strauss, and Giroux.

McDowell, John. 1994. *Mind and World.* Cambridge, MA: Harvard University Press.

Mill, John Stuart. 1952. *Autobiography.* Oxford: Oxford University Press.

——. 1962. *Utilitarianism, On Liberty, Essay on Bentham.* New York: New American Library.

Miller, William R., and C'de Baca, Janet. 2001. *Quantum Change.* New York: Guilford Press.

Mills, Cynthia. 2002. "Crashing the Culture Club," *Boston Globe*, November 26, C1, C3.

Miner, Valerie. 1993. "Writing and Teaching with Class," in Michelle M. Tokarczyk, and Elizabeth A. Fay, eds., *Working-Class Women in the Academy*. Amherst: University of Massachusetts Press, 73–86.

Montessori, Maria. 1964 (1912). *The Montessori Method*. New York: Schocken.

Mori, Kyoko. 1997. *Polite Lies*. New York: Fawcett Books.

Moses, Wilson J. 1993. "Ambivalent Maybe," in C. L. Barney Dews, and Carolyn Leste Law, eds., *This Fine Place So Far from Home*. Philadelphia: Temple University Press, 187–99.

Oakley, Ann. 1979. *Becoming a Mother*. Oxford: Martin Robertson & Co.

Odair, Sharon. 1993. "Vestments and Vested Interests: Academia, the Working Class, and Affirmative Action," in Michelle M. Tokarczyk, and Elizabeth A. Fay, eds., *Working-Class Women in the Academy*. Amherst: University of Massachusetts Press, 239–50.

Ortner, Sherry. 1974. "Is Female to Male as Nature Is to Culture?" In Michelle Zimbalist Rosaldo and Louise Lamphere, eds., *Women, Culture, and Society*. Palo Alto, CA: Stanford University Press, 67–87.

Orwell, George. 1984 (1953). "Such, Such Were the Joys," in *The Orwell Reader*. New York: Harcourt Brace.

Ovid. 1960. *The Metamorphoses*. New York: Mentor Books.

Park, Robert E. 1996 (1928). "Human Migration and the Marginal Man," in Werner Sollors, ed., *Theories of Ethnicity*. New York: Washington Square Press, 156–67.

Peckham, Irvin. 1993. "Complicity in Class Codes: The Exclusionary Function of Education," in C. L. Barney Dews, and Carolyn Leste Law, eds., *This Fine Place So Far from Home*. Philadelphia: Temple University Press, 263–76.

Pegueros, Rosa Maria. 1993. "*Todos Vuyelven*: From Potrero Hill to UCLA," in C. L. Barney Dews, and Carolyn Leste Law, eds., *This Fine Place So Far from Home*. Philadelphia: Temple University Press, 87–105.

Perry, Tony. 2004. "For Marine Snipers, War Is Up Close and Personal," *Boston Globe*, April 19, A10.

Peters, R. S. 1966. "Reason and Habit: The Paradox of Moral Education," in Israel Scheffler, ed., *Philosophy and Education*. Boston: Allyn and Bacon, 245–62.

———. 1967. "What Is an Educational Process?" in R. S. Peters, ed., *The Concept of Education*. New York: Humanities Press, 1–23.

———. 1972. "Education and the Educated Man," in R. F. Dearden and R. S. Peters, eds., *A Critique of Current Educational Aims*. London: Routledge and Kegan Paul.

Peterson, Susan Rae. 1984. "Against 'Parenting,'" in Joyce Trebilcot, ed., *Mothering*. Totowa, NJ: Rowman and Allenheld, 62–69.

Phillips, Donna Burns. 1993. "Past Voices, Present Speakers," in C. L. Barney Dews, and Carolyn Leste Law, eds., *This Fine Place So Far from Home*. Philadelphia: Temple University Press, 221–30.

Pinker, Steven. 1995. *The Language Instinct*. New York: Summit Books.

———. 2002. *The Blank Slate*. New York: Viking.

Plato. 1974. *Republic*. Trans. G. M. A. Grube. Indianapolis, IN: Hackett Publishing.

Rich, Adrienne. 1977. *Of Woman Born*. New York: Bantam Books.

Rodriguez, Richard. 1982. *Hunger of Memory*. Boston: David R. Godine.

———. 1992. *Days of Obligation*. New York: Penguin Books.

Rosenthal, Robert, and Jacobson, Lenore. 1968. *Pygmalion in the Classroom*. New York: Holt, Rinehart and Winston.

Rousseau, Jean-Jacques. 1979. *Emile*. Trans. Allan Bloom. New York: Basic Books.

Russell, Willy. 1985. *Educating Rita*. Essex: Longman Group.

Ryan, Jake, and Sackrey, Charles. 1984. *Strangers in Paradise*. Boston: South End Press.

Rymer, Russ. 1993. *Genie*. New York: Harper Collins.

Sacks, Oliver. 1989. *Seeing Voices*. Berkeley: University of California Press.

———. 1990. *Awakenings*. New York: HarperCollins.

Santayana, George. 1953. *The Life of Reason*. New York: Charles Scribner's.

Santiago, Esmeralda. 1998. *Almost a Woman*. New York: Vintage.

———. 2004. *The Turkish Lover*. New York: Da Capo Press.

Sartre, Jean Paul. 1956. "Existentialism Is a Humanism," in Walter Kaufman, ed., *Existentialism from Dostoevsky to Sartre*. New York: Meridian Books, 287–311.

Schaller, Susan. 1991. *A Man without Words*. New York: Summit Books.

Schwalbe, Michael. 1995. "The Work of Professing (A Letter to Home)," in C. L. Barney Dews, and Carolyn Leste Law, eds., *This Fine Place So Far from Home*. Philadelphia: Temple University Press, 309–31.

Sebold, Alice. 1999. *Lucky*. New York: Scribner.

Sege, Irene. 2005. "Student of Change," *Boston Globe*, October 19, F1, F8.

Shaw, George Bernard. 1963. *Complete Plays with Prefaces*. New York: Dodd, Mead and Company.

———. 1975. *Pygmalion*. New York: New American Library.

Silva, Christina M., and Raja Mishra. 2005. "Umpire's Call Gets Unheard-of Result," *Boston Globe*, July 30, 2005, B1, B4.

Singer, Isaac Bashevis. 1986. "Yentl the Yeshiva Boy," in Singer, *Short Friday*. New York: Fawcett, 159–92.

Smith, Patricia Clark. 1993. "Grandma Went to Smith, All Right, but She Went from Nine to Five: A Memoir," in Michelle M. Tokarczyk, and Elizabeth A. Fay, eds., *Working-Class Women in the Academy.* Amherst: University of Massachusetts Press, 126–39.

Stefansson, Anders H. 2004. "Sarajevo Suffering: Homecoming and the Hierarchy of Homeland Hardship," in Fran Markowitz and Anders H. Stefansson, eds., *Homecomings.* Lanham, MD: Lexington Books, 54–75.

Suárez-Orozco, Carola and Suárez-Orozco, Marcelo. 1995. *Trans-formations.* Palo Alto, CA: Stanford University Press.

Swofford, Anthony. 2003. *Jarhead.* New York: Scribner.

Tokarczyk, Michelle M., and Fay, Elizabeth A., eds. 1993. *Working-Class Women in the Academy.* Amherst: University of Massachusetts Press.

Tsuda, Takeyuki (Gaku). 2004. "When Home Is Not the Homeland: The Case of Japanese Brazilian Ethnic Return Migration," in Fran Markowitz and Anders H. Stefansson, eds., *Homecomings.* Lanham, MD: Lexington Books, 125–45.

Wakin, Daniel J. 2005. "Best Wishes on Your Job. Now Get Out," *New York Times,* October 9, 2005, AR1, AR31.

Walker, Alice. 1983. *In Search of Our Mothers' Gardens.* New York: Harcourt Brace and Company.

Warner, Marina. 2002. *Fantastic Metamorphoses, Other Worlds.* Oxford: Oxford University Press.

Washington, Booker T. 1965. *Up from Slavery,* in *Three Negro Classics.* New York: Avon Books.

Williams, Emlyn. 1938. *The Corn Is Green.* New York: Dramatists Play Service, Inc.

———. 1961. *George: An Early Autobiography.* New York: Random House.

Woodruff, William. 2003. *Beyond Nab End.* London: Abacus.

Woolf, Virginia. 1938. *Three Guineas.* New York: Harcourt, Brace, Jovanovich.

X, Malcolm. 1966. *The Autobiography of Malcolm X.* New York: Grove Press.

Yanne, L. 1997. "Zoos Are Teaching Children the Wrong Lessons," *Boston Globe,* February 6, A18.

Zimbardo, Rose. 1993. "Teaching the Working Woman," in Michelle M. Tokarczyk, and Elizabeth A. Fay, eds., *Working-Class Women in the Academy.* Amherst: University of Massachusetts Press, 208–15.

Zinn, Howard. 1994. *You Can't Get Off a Moving Train.* Boston: Beacon Press.

Acknowledgments

I owe a special debt of gratitude to the American Educational Studies Association for inviting me to give the 2002 George Kneller lecture. The enthusiastic response and probing questions of that Pittsburgh audience convinced me to make the paper I had written for the occasion[1] the springboard for a book about educational metamorphoses. My thanks go also to the students and colleagues who responded in kind when I subsequently presented that paper to the Research Seminar in Philosophy of Education of the London Institute of Education; the Philosophy of Education Society of Great Britain, West Midland Branch; the Society of Philosophy of Education of Tohoku University, Japan; and the University of Oklahoma as part of the College of Education's Diamond Anniversary Lecture Series. I also want to thank Jane Williams for reading my initial writeup of my case studies and encouraging me to go forward; Ann Diller, Susan Laird, Maurice Stein, and my dear departed friend Mary Woods for invaluable critiques of the first draft of this book; Ann Diller, Susan Franzosa, Barbara Houston, Susan Laird, Beatrice Nelson, Jennifer Radden, and Janet Farrell Smith for close readings of several chapters and lively conversations about the central ideas; and Michael Martin who encouraged me to write this book in the first place, patiently listened to every new idea of mine, and read the first and last drafts. I am especially grateful to Courtney Cazden for talking with me about a number of the issues concerning language learning that arise in Victor's case, Lani Guinier for giving me feedback on my discussion of her work, and Donaldo Macedo for allowing me to interview him. Hilde Hein also deserves special thanks for helping me find my editor, Ross Miller, whose faith in this project has meant a lot.

Also, I would like to acknowledge Paul Mahoney, an old friend who underwent an astounding educational metamorphosis right before my eyes long before I ever dreamed of writing a book on the topic. It was only after completing this volume that I remembered his case and realized that I was once a character in a story that closely resembles some of the ones that appear in these pages.

And finally, I gratefully acknowledge the permissions to reprint the following:

Excerpts from "Yentl, the Yeshiva Boy" from *The Collection Stories* by Isaac Bashevis Singer. Copyright © 1982 by Isaac Bashevis Singer. Reprinted by permission of Farrar, Straus and Giroux, LLC.

Excerpts from *The Autobiography of Malcom X* published by Hutchinson. Reprinted by permission of The Random House Group Ltd.

Excerpts from *The Autobiography of Malcolm X* by Malcolm X and Alex Haley. Copyright © 1964 by Alex Haley and Malcolm X. Copyright © 1965 by Alex Haley and Betty Shabazz. Used by permission of Random House, Inc.

Excerpts reprinted by permission of the publisher from *The Wild Boy of Aveyron* by Harlan Lane, pp. 10, 28, 100, 109, 155, 160, 166. Cambridge, Mass.: Harvard University Press, Copyright © 1976 by Harlan Lane.

Excerpts from *Educating Rita* by Willy Russell. Copyright © 1985 Methuen Publishing Limited.

Excerpts from *The Millstone* by Margaret Drabble. Copyright © 1965 Weidenfeld & Nicholson, an imprint of The Orion Publishing Group.

Excerpts from *The Millstone* by Margaret Drabble. Copyright © 1963 and renewed in 1993 by Margaret Drabble. Reprinted by permission of Harcourt, Inc.

Excerpts from *The Corn is Green* reprinted by permission of the author, Emlyn Williams.

NOTE

1. "Educational Metamorphoses," *Educational Studies*, vol. 35, no. 1 (February 2004), 7–24.

Index

About the Author

Jane Roland Martin, Ph.D., is professor of philosophy emerita at the University of Massachusetts, Boston. She is a recipient of a Guggenheim Fellowship and has been awarded honorary degrees in the United States and Sweden for her work in educational philosophy and theory. She is the author of seven other books, including *Reclaiming a Conversation*, *The Schoolhome*, and *Cultural Miseducation*, and over seventy-five articles and chapters in edited collections.